Cambridge Elements

Elements in The Aegean Bronze Age
edited by
Carl Knappett
University of Toronto
Irene Nikolakopoulou
Hellenic Ministry of Culture, Archaeological Museum of Heraklion

CLOTHING BODIES

Weaving and Textiles in the Aegean Bronze Age

Sophia Vakirtzi
Hellenic Ministry of Culture, HOCRED (ODAP)

CAMBRIDGE UNIVERSITY PRESS

Shaftesbury Road, Cambridge CB2 8EA, United Kingdom

One Liberty Plaza, 20th Floor, New York, NY 10006, USA

477 Williamstown Road, Port Melbourne, VIC 3207, Australia

314–321, 3rd Floor, Plot 3, Splendor Forum, Jasola District Centre, New Delhi – 110025, India

Cambridge University Press is part of Cambridge University Press & Assessment, a department of the University of Cambridge.

We share the University's mission to contribute to society through the pursuit of education, learning and research at the highest international levels of excellence.

www.cambridge.org
Information on this title: www.cambridge.org/9781009679091

DOI: 10.1017/9781009679084

© Sophia Vakirtzi 2026

This publication is in copyright. Subject to statutory exception and to the provisions of relevant collective licensing agreements, no reproduction of any part may take place without the written permission of Cambridge University Press & Assessment.

When citing this work, please include a reference to the DOI 10.1017/9781009679084

First published 2026

A catalogue record for this publication is available from the British Library

ISBN 978-1-009-67909-1 Hardback
ISBN 978-1-009-67910-7 Paperback
ISSN 2754-2998 (online)
ISSN 2754-298X (print)

Additional resources for this publication at www.cambridge.org/Vakirtzi

Cambridge University Press & Assessment has no responsibility for the persistence or accuracy of URLs for external or third-party internet websites referred to in this publication and does not guarantee that any content on such websites is, or will remain, accurate or appropriate.

For EU product safety concerns, contact us at Calle de José Abascal, 56, 1°, 28003 Madrid, Spain, or email eugpsr@cambridge.org

Clothing Bodies

Weaving and Textiles in the Aegean Bronze Age

Elements in The Aegean Bronze Age

DOI: 10.1017/9781009679084
First published online: February 2026

Sophia Vakirtzi
Hellenic Ministry of Culture, HOCRED (ODAP)
Author for correspondence: Sophia Vakirtzi, sophievak@gmail.com

Abstract: This Element explores the textile crafts and cloth cultures of the Aegean Bronze Age, focusing on two categories of archaeological evidence: excavated textiles (or their imprints) and tools used for yarn production and weaving. Together, these types of material testimonies offer complementary perspectives on a textile history that spans 2,000 years. A growing body of evidence suggests that the Aegean was home to communities of skilled textile craftspeople who produced cloth ranging from plain and coarse to fine and elaborate. As regional connectivity increased throughout the Bronze Age, interactions in textile craft flourished. In time, textile production became central to the political economies that emerged in the Aegean region. The expertise of Bronze Age Aegean spinners and weavers is vividly illustrated through the material record of their tools, while even the smallest excavated cloth fragments stand as fragile, yet enduring testaments to textile craftsmanship.

Keywords: archaeological textiles, textile craft, cloth cultures, textile tools, Aegean Bronze Age

© Sophia Vakirtzi 2026

ISBNs: 9781009679091 (HB), 9781009679107 (PB), 9781009679084 (OC)
ISSNs: 2754-2998 (online), 2754-298X (print)

Contents

1 Introduction   1

2 Background to Aegean Textiles Research   2

3 Weaving the Threads of Aegean Bronze Age Textile Histories   24

4 Overview of Aegean Bronze Age Textile Craft   71

5 Conclusion   74

   References   76

An online supplementary material is available at www.cambridge.org/Vakirtzi

1 Introduction

The Bronze Age Aegean provides us with nearly 2,000 years of textile history. Evidence of this history has long been found in various forms of material culture, since the early days of Aegean prehistoric research (e.g., Evans 1902, 55–58, Fig. 28, 102, Fig. 59; Paribeni 1908). Through the iconography of clothed human figures in the art of the second millennium BCE, a focus on garments and costume soon became possible. Archaeology of the early twentieth century was concerned with the distinction of Bronze Age 'ethnic' identities, and costume seemed an obvious basis for such categorizations (Myres 1950; Zora 1956). Since this early scholarship paid less attention to issues of production and craftsmanship, the study of cloth and textile craft fell behind the early focus on dress.[1]

From the mid twentieth century onwards, archaeology shifted towards a new paradigm, integrating the study of gender, economy, and technology. This had an impact on the study of Aegean Bronze Age textiles. Craftsmanship, gender and society became important research parameters. In Aegean prehistory, the study of dress iconography began to integrate a technological perspective, discussing the materials and techniques likely employed to manufacture the garments depicted in Aegean Bronze Age art (Sapouna-Sakellaraki 1971). These trends received a boost from the first, synthetic study of Aegean prehistoric textile tools (Carington Smith 1975), prompting attention to their systematic recording and collection. Moreover, textiles and textile production, seen as paradigmatic of a gendered division of labour, became analytical units in gender archaeology and a central theme in studies on female agency in history (Gero and Conkey 1991). The monumental work of E. W. Barber (1991), a milestone in the study of Aegean Bronze Age textiles, wove together all research traditions in a multifaceted and detailed treatment that transcended the geographic and chronological boundaries of the third and second millennia BCE Aegean. The social aspect of textile production was examined in the emblematic book by I. Tzachili (1997) through the case study of the Late Bronze Age (LBA) settlement of Akrotiri on Thera, within a gender archaeology perspective. Moreover, the emergence of experimental methodologies aiming at garment reconstruction (Jones 1998) paved the way for a more grounded understanding of Aegean Bronze Age dress.

Over the past twenty years, research on Aegean Bronze Age textiles has seen remarkable growth. Scholarship has been influenced especially by the Centre for Textile Research (CTR), University of Copenhagen, which has led the

---

[1] For semantic distinctions between the terms 'dress', 'clothing', and 'costume', see Roach-Higgins and Eicher 1992.

methodological advances in the study of textile tools from a functional perspective (Andersson Strand et al. 2022). As a result, many scholars have taken up studies of textile technology, contributing to an unprecedented accumulation and synthesis of data. Besides a fresh look on second-millennium-BCE dress, this approach allowed for insights into the craft of the third millennium BCE, a historical context largely left out of discussions on Bronze Age textiles in earlier scholarship, given the limited iconographic evidence of dress and a total lack of documentary testimonies from the Early Bronze Age (EBA). Another recent development is the emphasis put on the technological analysis of excavated textiles and textile imprints. Although the Aegean region is not favourable to the preservation of organic materials in archaeological deposits, it is increasingly observed that textiles can survive in special taphonomic environments. New and old textile finds are being (re)examined by a new generation of textile scholars specializing in archaeometric techniques. Their results provide a wealth of information on textile craft.

In this Element, an overview of Aegean Bronze Age textiles and textile craft is presented that prioritizes the research of the past twenty years, integrating older finds and reports when necessary. Thus, the focus is on the advances made through the study and analysis of textile tools and excavated textiles and textile imprints of the Early, Middle, and Late Bronze Ages (Table 1, Table 2). The datasets of textile tools are large and ever-expanding, so that a choice of the most well-studied cases or those providing exceptional insight, proved unavoidable (Map 1). This choice renders this Element a frame of reference rather than an exhaustive treatment of the subject. The main insights resulting from the rich body of work on textile and dress iconography will be briefly addressed in Section 2.2.1, with references to seminal, relevant scholarly works. Where deemed necessary, issues of cloth iconography will be raised within the discussions on textile technology.

2 Background to Aegean Textiles Research

2.1 Textile Craft: Basic Operations and Definitions

Textile production in a pre-industrial technological frame entails a long and time-consuming operational sequence. Its basic stages include the procurement of fibres harvested from plant and/or animal sources, followed by untangling, cleaning and washing the fibres; manufacturing and dying thread (or yarn); fabricating cloth through weaving or other techniques; adding finishing details such as decorative elements during or after weaving; and/or tailoring (Andersson Strand 2015). However, the archaeological visibility of any of these stages depends on the material residues of the manufacturing processes. In the frame

Table 1 Excavated textiles and textile imprints mentioned in the text. All chronological attributions are contextual except for those of Kadmeia and Lefkandi, which derive from radiocarbon dating. Imprints are indicated in *italics*.

	The Insular Region	Crete	The Mainland
Late Bronze Age–Late	Pylona, Rhodes, LBA IIIA-IIIB	Chania tomb, LM IIIB "Chieftain's Grave", Zafer Papoura, LM II-IIIA Unexplored Mansion, *Knossos, post-LM II*	Lefkandi, Euboea, C14-dated Granary, Mycenae, LH IIIC *Deiras, Argos, LH IIIA-IIIB* Dendra tomb 2, Argolid, LH IIIA Griffin Warrior tomb, Messenia, LH IIA Kazarma, Argolid, LH II
Late Bronze Age–Early	Akrotiri, Thera, LC IA	Kastelli, Chania, LM I Zakros, Lasithi, LM I	Grave Circle A, Mycenae, LH I Grave Circle B, Mycenae, MH III-LH I Eleon Boeotia, MH III- LH I
Middle Bronze Age	—	Malia, Herakleion, MM II	Kadmeia, Boeotia, C14-dated
Early Bronze Age	*Markiani, Amorgos, EC II-late* *Markiani, Amorgos, EC II-early* Dokathismata, Amorgos, EC II-early Akrotiri, Thera, EC II-early Akrotiri, Thera, EC II-early	—	*Geraki, Laconia, EH II*
Final Neolithic	*Vathy, Astypalaia, FN-EC I* Kephala, Kea, FN	—	—

Table 2 Thread count per sq. cm of the textiles/textile imprints mentioned in the text based on publication reports

Date	Threads per sq. cm	Preservation status/Provenance	Publication
C14-dated	19×19	Textile remains/Lefkandi, Euboea	Margariti & Spantidaki 2020
	20×80	Textile remains/Lefkandi, Euboea	Margariti & Spantidaki 2020
LH IIIA–IIIB	9–10×10	Imprints/Deiras, Argolid	Siennicka 2025
	14×16–18	Textile remains/Pylona, Rhodes	de Wild 2001
	16×18	Textile remains/Pylona, Rhodes	de Wild 2001
LC I/LM I	4–5×10	Textile remains/Kastelli, Chania	Möller-Wiering 2006
	4–5×10–12	Textile remains/Akrotiri, Thera	Spantidaki & Moulhérat 2021
	5–6×7	Textile remains/Akrotiri, Thera	Spantidaki & Moulhérat 2021
	20–22×20–22	Textile remains/Akrotiri, Thera	Spantidaki & Moulhérat 2021
MH III–LH I	20×22	Textile remains/Grave Circle B, Mycenae	Spantidaki & Moulhérat 2012
	4–5×7–16	Textile remains/Eleon, Boeotia	Burke & Dimova 2023
C14-dated	12–17×14–17	Textile remains/Kadmeia, Boeotia	Margariti & Spantidaki 2023b
MM II	20×20	Textile remains/Malia Crete	Cutler et al. 2013
EBA II–Early	8×25–30	Imprint/Geraki, Laconia	Vogelsang-Eastwood 1999
FN	9×11–12×14	Imprints/Kephala, Kea	Carington Smith 1977

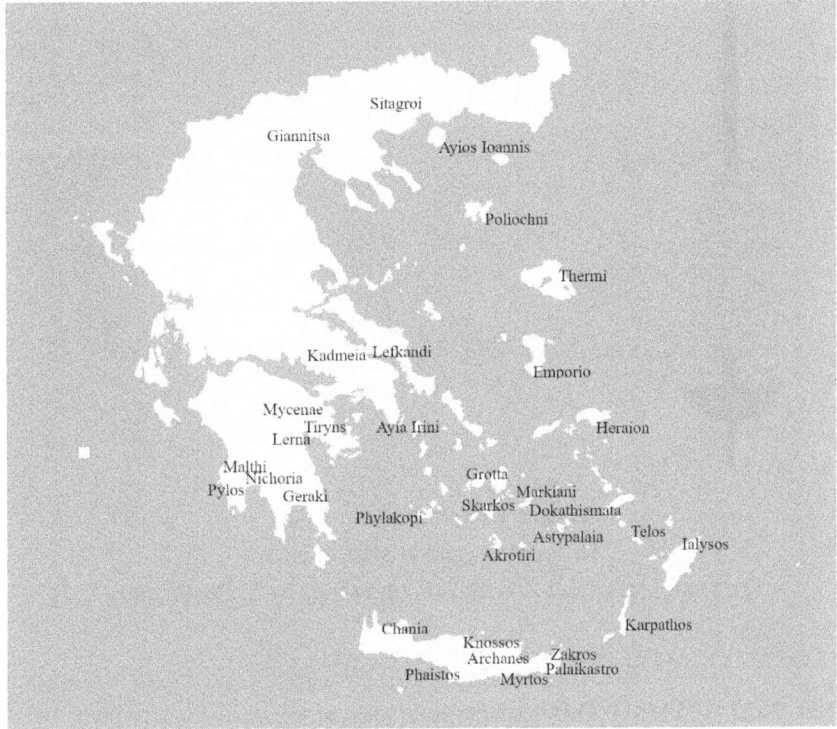

Map 1 Place names and sites mentioned in the text (map created by the author based on Google Maps).

of Aegean prehistory, the textile works most frequently represented in the archaeological record are manufacturing thread and weaving cloth, through the recovery of textile tools such as spindle whorls and loomweights.

A spindle whorl is an accessory to the spindle, a thin rod, used in the process of twisting fibres into thread, or for plying single threads into thicker ones. It has a simple function but its handling requires skill: the spinner draws a few fibres from a mass of raw material that is fixed on a distaff, attaches these to the tip of the rod, and twirls the spindle while continuously drawing some more fibres. As the rod rotates, the fibres are spun into thread, while the spinner continues 'feeding' the spindle, drafting more material from the distaff. The whorl, which has a circular shape, is fixed on the rod through its central perforation and with its weight reinforces the rotation of the spindle (Barber 1991, 56–59) (Figure 1a). The spinner stops once in a while to reel the spun thread onto the spindle, and then continues drafting fibres and twirling the spindle. This is called draft-spinning (Barber 1991, 41–51). Ethnographic documentation indicates that there exist various technical gestures for handling the spindle in draft-spinning (Vakirtzi

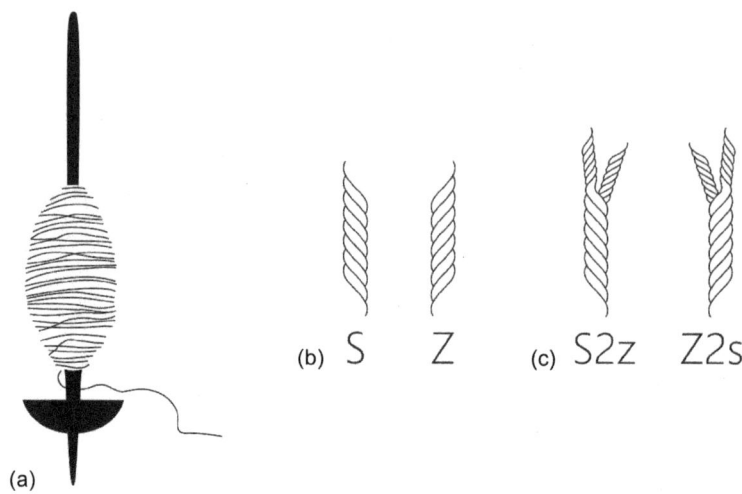

Figure 1a Spindle with whorl.
1b Single s- and z-twist threads.
1c Double S2z and Z2s threads (drawings by V. Papazikou).

et al. 2022, 175–181). Different gestures may result in distinct primary twist direction, which is conventionally defined with the letters *z* or *s*, in accordance with the central slant of these two letters (Figure 1b). E. Barber suggested that a general correlation among direction of primary twist, spinning gesture (suspended or supported spindle), choice of spindle (low or high whorl) and fibre type can be made: z-twist has been associated with suspended, low-whorl spindles and wool, while flax is correlated to high-whorl spindles rolled on the spinners' thighs (Barber 1991, 65–68). However, the more ancient textile analysis progresses, accumulating fresh data, the more Barber's proposed correlation deserves re-evaluation. The combination of two z-twist threads into a secondary, plied one, manifests a secondary S-twist and is ascribed as S2z. Similarly, two primary s-twist threads plied together will result in a Z2s structure (Skals et al. 2015, 62) (Figure 1c). A different technique of thread manufacture has been observed in excavated textiles, called splicing. Splicing entails joining individual fibres of plant origin, either continuously along their length or end to end, and then twisting them at their joints (or splices). Spliced threads are then twisted to create a stronger, plied thread, using the spindle (Barber 1991, 47, Fig. 2.9; Gleba and Harris 2019). Depending on the method of manufacture, the threads manifest certain structural features. Spun threads have continuous twists all along their length. Spliced threads demonstrate minimal to no twist, but the joints between fibres may sometimes be distinguished. Because both techniques require the use of the spindle, it is difficult to ascribe ancient whorls straightforwardly to either, although in general splicing is associated with heavier rather than lighter spindle whorls (see Section 2.2.2).

Cloth can be produced with various techniques, such as plaiting, twining or felting (Emery 1966), but in this Element the focus will be on weaving. This operation, at its most basic version, consists of interlacing two different thread systems – one passive and one active – at a right angle to each other. The threads of one system must be taut, while the threads of the other system are passed over and under them. These are called warps and wefts, respectively. Cross-culturally, several solutions were invented to keep the warp threads taut. These solutions correspond to different loom types. Two of the most well-known ones, the horizontal ground loom and the vertical loom, were certainly in use in the prehistoric Eastern Mediterranean and in the Near East (Barber 1991, 81–90). The vertical loom had two basic varieties, the two-beam and the warp-weighted variety, the latter being our main interest in this Element, since it is the only type of loom securely identified from the Bronze Age Aegean, through the recovery of loomweights. We gain glimpses to their function through archaic and classical art (Barber 1991, 110–113): these looms were constructed by two vertical supporting beams and an upper horizontal one, where the warp threads were tied to, or were let hanging from a 'starting border', a narrow strip of cloth. The lower ends of the warp threads were tied to loomweights that kept them taut so that weavers could pass in the weft threads, as vase paintings indicate (Supplementary Figure 1) (available to access at www.cambridge.org/Vakirtzi). They were also equipped with one or more wooden sticks or bars, called shed and heddle bars, to facilitate the mechanical opening of the warp threads and the faster passing of the weft (Barber 1991, Fig. 3.28). However, the exact structure of the Bronze Age Aegean warp-weighted loom is unknown. Nonetheless, it has been suggested that certain signs of the Linear A script such as *AB54* (Figure 2) must have been inspired by the warp-weighted loom (Del Freo et al. 2010, 351).

Warp-weighted looms can be used to create several different kinds of fabric structures (or weaves).[2] In the simplest weave, one thread system passes over and under the threads of the other system. This is called plain or tabby. It may have several variations. In the variety of 'balanced' plain weave, the warps and the wefts have approximately the same count per square centimetre (sq. cm) (Figure 3a). When the threads of the warp system are considerably more than those of the weft system, and vice versa, then the weave is 'faced', described as warp faced or weft faced, respectively (Figure 3b). A more complex

---

[2] In this text, the noun 'weave' is used to denote types of fabric structures resulting from different ways of interlacing at least two sets of structuring elements, following Emery 1966, 74–75 and Barber 1991, 126.

Figure 2 Schematic drawing of the Linear A sign *AB* 54 (drawing by V. Papazikou after Del Freo et al. 2010, Fig. 17.11).

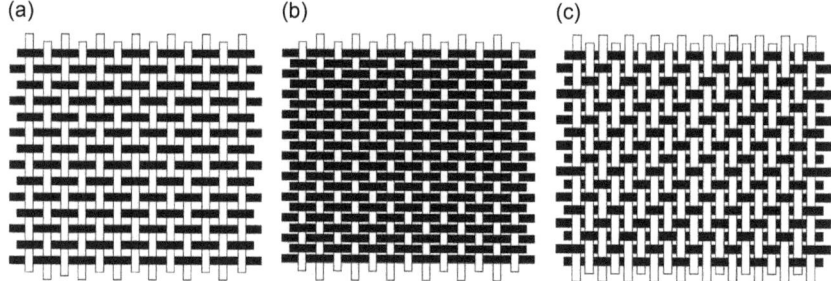

Figure 3a Plain (tabby), balanced weave.
b Plain (tabby) weft-faced weave.
c Twill (diagonal) 2/1 weave (drawings by V. Papazikou).

configuration is the diagonal weave, or 'twill', where the weft passes alternately over a number of warps and then under a different number of warps (Figure 3c). More sophisticated weaves combine the plain (or tabby) structure with supplementary or floating warp or weft threads inserted by the weaver by hand in the basic (or 'ground') fabric, or thread-looping techniques, to create decorative patterns. Tapestry is a more complex structure, developed primarily for creating coloured patterns by inserting discontinuous weft threads of different colours in the weave, following a predetermined design, and is, by definition, a weft-faced type of textile (Emery 1966, 78; Vogelsang-Eastwood 2000, 278). Tapestries from the Bronze Age Eastern Mediterranean have been found in Egypt (Vogelsang-Eastwood 2000; Spinazzi-Lucchesi 2018), where they are associated to the emergence of the artistic representation of the two-beam loom, and in Syria (Andersson Strand and Nosch 2015, Appendix B, with references). Moreover, tapestry is presumably implied by some textile terms found in the Old Assyrian records of Kanesh dating to the nineteenth century BCE (Smith 2013, 162, with references). All types of weaves can be further elaborated by fringes, tassels, embroideries and other techniques (Barber 1991, 126–144, 166–174).

2.2 Sources of Textile Evidence from the Bronze Age Aegean and Methodologies of Research

2.2.1 Cloth Representations

The depiction of clothed human figures in Aegean Bronze Age art is one of the most important sources of textile iconography, thus the discourse on textiles is often conflated with the discourse on dress. For half of the period under discussion, specifically the EBA or the third millennium BCE, the iconographic record related to cloth is limited. The representation of the human body in the art of this period is mostly rendered in three-dimensional figurines modelled either in clay or in stone and less frequently in bone or metal (Marangou 1992). Regardless of region, material, or stylistic tradition, scholars have observed that EBA figurines rarely incorporate iconographic details that can be informative on clothing and textiles (Marangou 1992, 189–190; Mina 2008, 87).

The naturalistic marble Cycladic figurines and their Cycladicizing counterparts, dating from the EBA II onwards, mostly give the impression of the naked human body. Exceptions include figures with sculpted hats or narrow cross-bands worn on the torso to carry weapons such as daggers (Mina 2008, 87). However, these bands could have well been manufactured from leather and are not certain to represent textiles. A few clay figurines from this period often bear painted or incised motifs that have been interpreted as clothing items like caps, belts and bands worn around the waist or the hips, as well as cross-bands over the chest (Mina 2008, 87). Examples include figurines from Lerna with painted cross-bands on the torso, areas hatched with parallel lines or belts on the waist (Banks 1967, 643, Pl. 20; Marangou 1992, 190, Fig. 81) and from Thermi on the island of Lesbos, in the East Aegean, dated from the Third town onwards (Philaniotou 2019, 146). Some of the Thermi figurines bear incised motifs that have been interpreted as dress items (Figure 4), such as a fringed string tied in a knot behind the neck, cross-bands on the chest and a hip-long garment

Figure 4 Clay female figurine, from Thermi, Lesbos
(Lamb 1928/29–1929/30, Pl. XX, 29–1, image reproduced with permission of
The British School at Athens).

with fringes hanging from its hem on the waist and hips, with punctured dots that were suggested to depict embroidery (Lamb 1928–1929/1929–1930, 31–32, Pl. VIII). In Crete, a class of anthropomorphic clay vessels dating from the Early Minoan (EM) II to the Middle Minoan (MM) IA includes examples that bear painted motifs (Figure 5). Such vessels with painted hatched triangles or rectangles, or elaborate horizontal and vertical bands, are published from the EM settlement of Myrtos (Warren 1972, Plates 69–70), from Koumasa, Mochlos, Malia (Warren 1973, with references) and Phourni-Archanes (Sakellarakis and Sapouna-Sakellaraki 1997, 540–541). These anthropomorphic vessels have been considered as representations of female deities wearing elaborate dress (Warren 1973). However, Jones (2015, 13–22) rejects the interpretation of the painted motifs as garment depictions, arguing that they are typical, decorative patterns on EM non-anthropomorphic pottery.

Other artistic media with presumed dress iconography from the transitional period between the third and second millennia BCE include some Cretan figurines made of bone, stone, and metal, as well as figures carved on Cretan seals. Two figurines made of hippopotamus ivory and another made of marble, found in the Hagios Charalambos cave in the Lasithi area, East Crete, and attributed to the EM III-MM IA period, have body shapes that lack a clear distinction of the legs and have thus been considered as clothed in cloaks or long

Figure 5 Clay anthropomorphic rhyton, from Malia, Crete (inv. nr. Π8665 ©Archaeological Museum of Heraklion/ODAP/Hellenic Ministry of Culture).

dresses (Ferrence 2017). A metal anthropomorphic figurine from Archanes, dating to the end of the Prepalatial or the beginning of the Protopalatial period, was cast in a shape that suggests a foot-length garment (Sakellarakis and Sapouna-Sakellaraki 1997, 527). It was interpreted as a male 'wearing female dress' by the excavators (Sakellarakis and Sapouna-Sakellaraki 1997, 527) but was considered as a female wearing a bell-shaped skirt by Stefani (2013, 47–54). Some representations of clothing are also encountered on figurines and seals found in funerary contexts from the Tholos Tombs of Mesara, like the ivory female figurine from Platanos, with a long skirt bordered by parallel bands on the hem (Stefani 2013, 49), and the ivory seal from Archanes depicting a female figure with a long dress and a high collar, known as the 'Medicis Collar' (Sakellarakis and Sapouna-Sakellaraki 1997, 675–676).

In the course of the Middle Bronze Age, the representation of human clothing found new expression in Cretan art. The anthropomorphic clay figurines found in large quantities in peak sanctuaries render both female and male dress: long, bell-shaped or pleated skirts with wide belts tied in elaborate knots and various types of hats for women (Stefani 2013, 55–79), as well as various types of loincloths and belts for men (Sapouna-Sakellaraki 1971, 7–29; Rehak 1996, 42–43). The details of patterned cloth did not escape the attention of figurine makers: the painted bands on the garments of female figurines from Petsofas (Supplementary Figure 2) is one such case, probably corresponding to colour-patterning. Such patterning has been suggested to be the result of either weaving with supplementary weft techniques or of sewing narrow bands on the hems of skirts (Stefani 2013, 60).

While these developments in representational art were underway on Crete, human imagery was rare in the Middle Bronze Age art of the Greek Mainland and in the rest of the insular Aegean (Tzonou-Herbst 2012, 215). Pictorial art is largely lacking from the Middle Helladic (MH) material culture (Blakolmer 2010), rendering the clothing of this period archaeologically invisible. In the insular region, human representation is rare, schematic and mostly confined to vase painting. For example, at Akrotiri, Thera, the human figure as a theme in vase painting of the early second millennium BCE (Doumas 2018) provides few clues to dress of the Middle Cycladic (MC) period. A few anthropomorphic figures depicted on local pottery sherds are rendered in hourglass shape (Nikolakopoulou 2019, 276, Fig. 3.2), indicating, at best, knee-length garments (kilts?) (Figure 6). Slightly later, but still in the MC period and locally produced, is an exceptional bichrome jug with a 'pouring scene', depicting two males dressed in 'Minoan cloth' (Nikolakopoulou 2019, Vol. I, 282, Fig. 3.8, Vol. II, 230).

The artistic landscape changed radically in the period marked by the emergence of the New Palaces on Crete, towards the end of the Middle Bronze Age, in the MM III phase. Along with the art of wall-painting, eventually adopted in the Cyclades and the mainland, a rich iconography of clothing emerged, and one that now represented elaborately patterned, multicoloured textiles. Moreover,

Figure 6 Pottery sherd with painted schematic male figures, from Akrotiri, Thera (Doumas 2018, 31, Fig. 4 c)
(©Akrotiri Excavations/ODAP/The Athens Archaeological Society).

Figure 7 Girl with patterned flounced skirt and bodice, covering her figure with a crocus-coloured, red-dotted, transparent, long veil. Detail from 'The Adorants' Fresco, Xeste 3, from Akrotiri, Thera (©Akrotiri Excavations/The Athens Archaeological Society).

anthropomorphic figurines crafted in metal, ivory, stone or clay, and developments in glyptic, enrich the sources of cloth iconography. These artistic representations showcase a wide range of garments, including various types of skirts (bell-shaped, flounced, fringed, pleated, with horizontal bands), as well as pants, loincloths, kilts, mantles, long robes with diagonal bands, tight bodices with narrow hem-bands and tassels, aprons, belts and hats (Figures 7–8, Supplementary Figures 3–4). Among these are also items such as knots, scarves and cloaks or garments that are depicted either independently of human figures or as being carried by them, presumably with a symbolic or cult significance (Figure 9, Supplementary Figure 5). Given the identification of the narrated themes or episodes, these dresses and individual cloth items have been characterized as prestige, ritual or sacred (Crowley 2012; Boloti 2014; Jones 2015; Blakolmer 2018). Colours, ornamental styles, decorative techniques, embroidery, tailoring and sewing, as well as regional fashions, have been identified in

Figure 8 Male figures in procession, wearing colourful, patterned kilts. Detail from the 'Procession Fresco', from Knossos, Crete (inv. nr. T3 ©Archaeological Museum of Heraklion/ODAP/Hellenic Ministry of Culture).

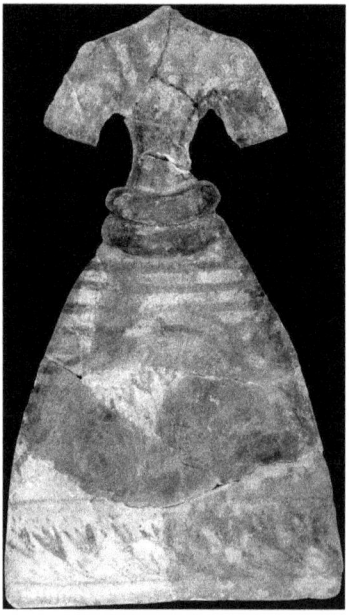

Figure 9 Faience replica of a dress composed by a long skirt decorated with crocuses, a double belt and a tight bodice, from the Temple Repositories, Knossos, Crete (inv. nr. 58 ©Archaeological Museum of Heraklion/ODAP/ Hellenic Ministry of Culture).

the dress imagery of the LBA (Barber 1991, 312–357; Stefani 2013). Research has suggested a distinction between 'Minoan' and 'Mycenaean' garments, based on this corpus of representations. For example, characteristic types of 'Minoan' female dress include the 'fleece' or 'animal-hide' skirt; the 'bell-shaped skirt' and the 'flounced' skirt combined with the tight bodice; and several types of pants and headdresses, most of which appear to be richly patterned (Stefani 2013). 'Mycenaean' female dress, in contrast, is represented by an 'all covering chemise' of less elaborate decoration (Barber 1991, 315) or a 'long robe' with bands on the hem, and often with a vertical band as well (Boloti 2014). Nonetheless, a degree of influence and hybridization between the two cloth-culture spheres has been acknowledged, best expressed in the multi-figured scene painted on the LM III sarcophagus of Ayia Triada, Crete: the types of garments worn by female and male actors within the same ritual episode include both Cretan and mainland elements (Burke 2005; Boloti 2014).

Textile patterns as depicted in LBA dress iconography have received a special focus from scholars. A variety of elaborate and detailed floral and geometric motifs, and in a few cases figurative ones, too (Barber 1991, 317–321) appear to have been embellishing the textiles that were tailored into female and male garments. Some of these patterns are not exclusive in the depiction of dress. Wall-painting and vase painting share in this rich repertoire of motifs as well (e.g., Betancourt 2007; Hatzaki 2018). Careful observation of the iconographic details of these garments and textiles supports theories on the artistic conventions employed to render different cloth textures. Cases in point are the 'transparent' dress items and the 'fleece' or 'animal-hide' skirts. Transparent textiles are identified when the contours of a garment contain the depiction of other items of clothing, or of the arms and legs of human figures, suggesting visibility beneath the cloth (Stefani 2013, 109–110). The 'fleece' or 'animal-hide' skirt, first attested in ceramic vase painting of Protopalatial Phaistos, recurring in Neopalatial seals and last represented on the Ayia Triada sarcophagus mentioned earlier (Stefani 2013, 104–107), conveys a 'woolly' impression. This was suggested to reflect weft-looping (Tzachili 1997, 242–243), a technique which involves loosely twining supplementary wefts around the warps in a way that leaves small loops hanging on the surface of the woven cloth. This technique survives on actual cloth fragments found in Middle Kingdom Egypt (Vogelsang-Eastwood 2000, 276).

Besides human dress, LBA iconography informs us on the use of products such as sailcloth, strings, ropes, and nets for captivating animals (e.g., Doumas 1992, Papageorgiou 2021, Betancourt 2007). These fibre-based artefacts are created with the same manufacturing principles and materials that are also used for weaving cloth for garments. Thus, their study adds important layers of information for a broader understanding of textile crafts (Vakirtzi et al. 2018).

2.2.2 Textile Tools and Production Facilities

The most frequently occurring tools in Aegean Bronze Age archaeological deposits are the remains of spindles and warp-weighted looms, namely spindle whorls and loomweights (Barber 1991; Tzachili 1997). Other textile implements found in Bronze Age sites include needles made of bone or metal, spinning bowls, that is, a type of clay bowl used for plying thread, pointy bone tools usually identified as pin beaters and pierced spools which have been interpreted as reels possibly related to warping. Throughout the Bronze Age, spindle whorls and loomweights were manufactured in a variety of shapes and sizes (Figures 10–11) and with materials such as clay, stone, or bone. Established tool typologies (Carington Smith 1975; Andersson Strand and Nosch 2015) facilitate the identification of these objects in the field, but certain types of ambiguous objects are more difficult to identify as implements related to textile craft (Barber 1991, 91–93).

Textile tools lend themselves to an array of analytical approaches. The most widely applied are distribution, typological, and functional analysis. Recently, the potential of clay provenance studies applied in textile tools analysis has been highlighted (Gorogianni et al. 2015; Vakirtzi 2019), which is especially promising in demonstrating the 'mobility' of textile craftspeople (Cutler 2021, 258). Another important aspect of textile tools study calls for collaboration with Aegean specialists in administration technologies, including stamping, marking and writing, because in certain cases Aegean Bronze Age textile tools bear traces of these practices on their surfaces (e.g., Vlasaki and Hallager 1995; Burke 2003; Tzachili 2007a; Burke 2010, 57; Evely 2012; Militello 2014b, 276; Cutler 2016b, 178; Karnava 2018, 162, 166; Karnava 2019, 502, with

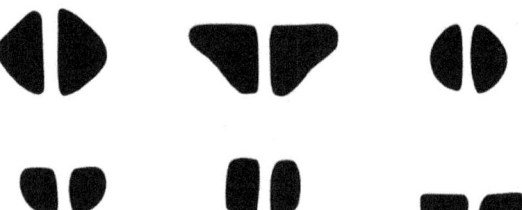

Figure 10 Basic spindle whorl types from Bronze Age Aegean sites. From left to right, upper row: biconical, conical, spherical. Lower row: hemispherical, cylindrical, discoid (drawings by S. Vakirtzi).

Clothing Bodies

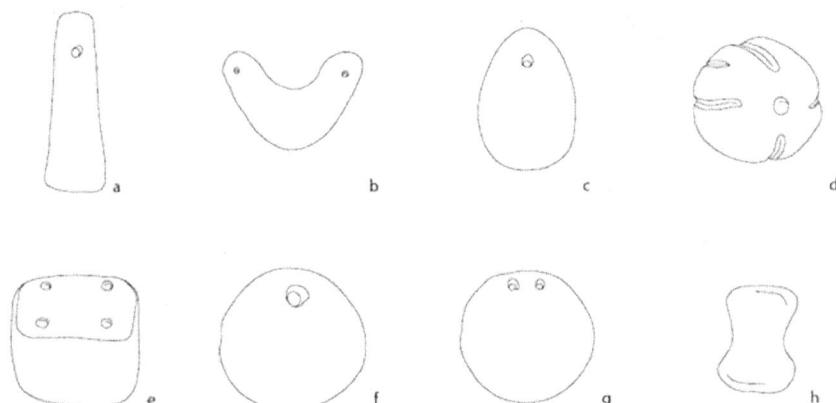

Figure 11 Basic loomweight types from Bronze Age Aegean sites. Upper row: (a) pyramidal, (b) crescent-shaped, (c) piriform, (d) spherical, (e) cuboid, (f) round discoid with one perforation, (g) round discoid with two perforations, (h) spool-shaped (drawings by V. Papazikou).

references; Tzigounaki and Karnava 2020, 324; Siennicka 2020; Cutler 2021, 145, 238). These practices are not yet well understood in terms of the relation between textile craft and the use of administration technology or the extent of Bronze Age 'literacy'.

Distribution analysis permits the interpretation of the spatial configuration of tools found in archaeological deposits. On a first level, it aims to distinguish between secondary deposits such as backfills, destruction debris, or building materials where textile tools often end up after being broken and disposed of, and primary deposits implying use spaces, intentional deposition related to funerary customs or other special behavioural patterns (see Section 3.4). On a second level, when textile tools are found in primary deposition in use spaces, their distribution patterns may reveal the organization and scale of production. Distribution analysis may also allow the distinction between loomweights in storage and loomweights fallen from a set-up loom (see Section 3.4.3).

Typological analysis, a conventional archaeological methodology, has enabled the distinction between different manufacturing choices with regard to the shape and size of spindle whorls and loomweights. The first comprehensive survey of Aegean prehistoric textile tools, conducted by J. Carington Smith (1975), led to the development of a detailed typology that remains a point of reference to this day. The attribution of textile tools to distinct types permits the comparison of different assemblages, ultimately allowing to discern patterns of continuity and changes in the habits of tool manufacture at the site level. Typological classification is also the basis of identifying regional interactions or influences among distinct communities of textile craftspeople, after mapping the various types of tools in geographical space. An example of this approach can be seen in the suggestion that the hollow ('scodelletta') spindle whorl type indicates the mobility of craftspeople over large spans of space and time (Barber 1991, 299–310, see Section 3.1.1).

Functional analysis aims at interpreting the functional potential of textile tools. It is a method developed at the CTR aiming to correlate the tool shape and size with its intended function to produce specific results. In the case of loomweights, it is based on weaving experiments that demonstrated that the tools' thickness and weight are important functional attributes (Mårtensson et al. 2009). They influence the loom setup, that is, how densely-spaced the warp threads are, and also the types of threads (fine, medium, coarse) and how many threads can be attached to each loomweight (Olofsson et al. 2015, 89–92). Thus, when archaeologists record the weight and thickness of loomweights found in archaeological deposits, they provide data that is essential to suggest potential loom setups, and eventually fabric types that could have been produced with a given yarn quality (Olofsson et al. 2015, 95–97). The CTR team applied functional analysis to a large sample of Aegean Bronze Age loomweights and suggested that the metrological variation of textile tools reflects not simply preferences in loomweight design, but most probably corresponding preferences in different cloth types (Andersson Strand and Nosch 2015, 362–371). For example, it was demonstrated that when producing plain (tabby) weaves, thick loomweights are optimal for weaving 'open' fabrics, that is, cloth with loosely distanced warp threads, whereas thin loomweights are optimal for denser cloth (Andersson Strand 2015b, 143). Nevertheless, this method has its limits in reconstructing the end-product. The weave structure and the overall appearance of the finished fabric are not defined only by warp threads. Among other factors, the arrangement of weft threads also plays an important role in the final appearance of cloth, determining if the weave is balanced or not. For example, open weaves can be filled in by multiple counts of wefts, creating weft-faced fabrics. An important result of the research conducted by the CTR team is the suggestion that despite the wide range of loomweight types of the Bronze Age Aegean, several overlap in a functional sense. This means that although they have a different shape, some loomweights can yield similar results. The loomweight types that are clearly distinct from a functional perspective and would thus have been used for the production of different types of textiles are the spherical, the pyramidal, and the discoid (Andersson Strand and Nosch 2015, 371). Based on this assessment, it can be suggested that, although the warp-weighted loom technology was shared by craft communities in different regions of the Bronze Age Aegean, the cloth produced by these communities may have been considerably different from one place to the other. For example, when comparing weaving with pyramidal loomweights at EBA Sitagroi, northern Greece (Elster 2003), to weaving with discoid loomweights at EBA Myrtos, southern Crete (Warren 1972), it can be argued that, although both of these communities used the warp-weighted loom technology, their sense of textiles must have been very different, when considering the different functional potential that pyramidal and discoid loomweights have.

In the case of spindle whorls, scholars have been debating what constitutes the most crucial functional attributes that determine their effect on the spinning or plying process, and ultimately on the quality of the produced thread (Vakirtzi et al. 2022, 181–184). Nonetheless, there is general consensus that their weight is an approximate indication of the quality of fibres and the thread thickness (Andersson Strand and Nosch 2015, 359–362). In this rationale, significantly different spindle whorls, in terms of their weight, would be used to manufacture significantly different thread types. Fine yarns generally require well-processed, fine fibres to be spun with a spindle equipped with a light whorl. The manufacture of thick, single threads or plied ones requires using a heavier whorl. Spinning experiments conducted by the CTR have confirmed that the weight of the whorl can be indicative of the thickness of the thread, but it cannot be diagnostic of the fibre source, that is, the plant or animal species (Olofsson et al. 2015). It has also been suggested that the whorl's diameter affects the speed of rotation of the spindle, and therefore influences how loosely or densely spun the thread will be (Barber 1991, 53; Olofsson 2015, 33; Olofsson et al. 2015, 87). Thus, for a functional analysis of spindle whorls, the first step requires recording the metric data of these tools, especially the weight and diameter values (Andersson Strand and Nosch 2015, passim). By projecting these on a weight-diameter scatterplot, it is possible to demonstrate the frequencies of whorls of different sizes in the sample of tools under study, and to compare patterns of thread production in general, qualitative terms (e.g., Andersson Strand and Nosch 2015, passim; Vakirtzi 2020).

2.2.3 Excavated Textiles and Textile Imprints

Textiles are repositories of a wealth of information on textile craft, ranging from fibre economy to textile technology, to styles and fashion. Depending on the degree of preservation of excavated textiles, the diagnosis of fibre type, thread-making technology, weave structure or pigments, may be possible, using an array of analytical instruments and physicochemical techniques (Margariti et al. 2024). In the Aegean region textiles have survived in archaeological deposits usually following carbonization, mineralization, or calcification (Spantidaki and Margariti 2017, 51). These are three distinct chemical processes, each triggered by specific pre-depositional or post-depositional conditions. Each of these processes alters the original chemical composition, appearance, and tactile effect of the textiles but at the same time prevents the activity of bacteria that cause the degradation of organic matter.

Excavated textiles can be observed using simple magnifying lenses or optical microscopy to determine the type of weave and to record the density of warp and weft threads in terms of thread count per sq. cm. Special features can also be recognized under low magnification, like the use of supplementary threads for decoration (e.g., embroidery, knotting) or reinforcement of the ground weave (e.g., in hems or selvedges) and even weaving mistakes (Carington Smith 1977). The compilation of such information can help identify techniques of weaving and distinguish patterns of preferred weave types, when plotting a large statistical sample in space and time (e.g., Gleba 2017). In the case of the Aegean region (including Mainland Greece), almost all extant textiles and textile imprints dating to the Bronze Age demonstrate plain (tabby) weave, in several variations (Spantidaki and Moulhérat 2012; Spantidaki and Moulhérat 2021).

Thread-making technology can be deduced by observing threads or their imprints under high magnification. Spinning can be securely identified as the manufacturing technique when twists are observed all along the length of a thread. In contrast, when minimal twist is present, it is more probable that the technique of splicing had been used (Gleba and Harris 2019), even if the splices (the joints between individual fibres) are difficult to trace. In the case of spun threads, microscopic observation facilitates the examination of thread structure (single or double/plied) and technical details such as the direction of twist or the twist angle. Average thread diameter and spin direction of thread groups are important when attempting to discern between potentially different textiles found tangled together in an archaeological deposit. However, it should be kept in mind that all measurements taken from archaeological threads and fibres should be interpreted with caution, since experiments have shown that the original dimensions of threads can be distorted following carbonization, mineralization or other processes taking place after the deposition of textiles in the soil (Margariti 2020).

Fibre identification can be attempted with the SEM and Optical microscopes, each type providing certain advantages and constraints for ancient textile analysis (Lukesova and Holst 2024). Details of fibre anatomy in mineralized and carbonized textile fragments can be observed under large magnification achieved with the SEM, provided that diagnostic anatomical features have been preserved. At the most basic level, analysis aims to distinguish between cellulosic and proteinaceous fibres, that is, those of plant and animal origin respectively. This is possible due to the distinct anatomical features exhibited by each of these two fibre categories (Rast-Eicher 2016, 11–42): in general, plant fibres are characterized by nodes along their length, while the surface of animal fibres is configured as small, pointy scales. To specify further the animal or plant species that had been sourced for their fibres, it is necessary to identify further morphological details, or to collect metric data that help distinguish among potential sources, based on a comparison of the archaeological fibres with those in reference collections (Rast-Eicher 2016). Physicochemical methods for fibre identification include various techniques. Among those, Fourier-Transform Infrared (FTIR) Microspectroscopy, aiming at the definition of the chemical composition of the textile fragments, has been applied on Aegean material; however, the method is not suitable for carbonized textile fragments (Spantidaki and Margariti 2017, 52). Recently, proteomics analysis has gained momentum in textile archaeology, as a new method of identifying animal textile fibres (Solazzo 2019; Andersson Strand et al. 2022, 23). Studies aiming at textile fibre identification based on these advanced methods promise significant breakthroughs in our knowledge of prehistoric fibre economies.

Extant textiles are also potential sources of information on textile dyes when textile fragments preserve traces of colour. Dyes can be detected and chemically defined with spectrophotometric analytical techniques, such as High-Performance Liquid-Chromatography (HPLC) (Vanden Berghe 2013). Moreover, being organic materials, excavated textiles can be radiocarbon-dated (Margariti et al. 2023a).

Another source of information on textile craft is provided by the imprints of woven or plaited cloth and threads or strings, depending on the quality of the impression. They occur on clay (Carington Smith 1977; Vakirtzi et al. 2018; Ulanowska 2020), soil (Unruh 2007; Vlachopoulos 2024, 667–674, Figs. 11–12), plaster (Egan 2015; Vakirtzi et al. 2018), and fine metal foil (Konstantinidi-Syvridi 2014, 148–151, Fig. 6.15–6.17). They are created either with intentional pressure on a malleable, plastic surface, or by chance, retaining negative impressions of the original thread and cloth structures. Textile imprints analysis can yield information on thread and weave structures but they are not optimal for investigating fibre sources, since the microscopic diagnostic features of fibre anatomy will not leave any impression on clay, plaster, or soil. Nonetheless, the experimental creation and documentation of imprints of threads and strings made of various raw materials have the potential to facilitate the identification of fibres in archaeological imprints, after comparison with the experimental ones (Ulanowska 2020). In considering textile imprints in this Element, only woven structures will be discussed, the imprints of threads and strings being too numerous to present here. A thorough documentation of thread and string imprints on clay sealings of the Bronze Age Aegean can be found in the database that resulted from the research project 'Textiles and Seals' directed by A. Ulanowska (https://textileseals.uw.edu.pl/database-description/).

2.2.4 Bioarchaeological Remains of Resources Related to Textile Raw Materials

Indirect evidence for the use of textile raw materials, such as fibres and dyes, may derive from bioarchaeological research. Zooarchaeological and archaeobotanical studies targeting, among other things, the analysis of faunal remains such as ovicaprid bones, and seeds or other parts of plants respectively, may produce results indicative of husbandry and agricultural regimes compatible with wool harvesting, flax cultivation, or other strategies for fibre collection. The detection of flax seeds in Bronze Age contexts (Valamoti 2011) supports the hypothesis of flax cultivation, one of its probable uses having been for textile production. Sheep and goat bones are commonly found in faunal assemblages, potentially indicating wool production (Halstead and Isaakidou 2011, 67–68). The moth cocoon of an insect that produces wild silk, found in an urban context in the Late Cycladic (LC) settlement of Akrotiri, Thera, has prompted a discussion on the possible use of wild silk as textile fibre (Panagiotakopulu et al. 1997). Pina shells found in several Bronze Age sites indicate the possible exploitation of sea silk (Burke 2012; Soriga and Carannante 2017). Heaps of *Hexaplex trunculus* (murex) shells point to the production of purple dye (Ruscillo 2005), known to have been used in textile production.

2.2.5 Textual Sources

The corpus of Mycenaean documents written in the Linear B script, spanning a period of about 200 years, is an important source of information on textile economy and craft. These texts are records of the 'palatial' administration of economic resources, raw materials, people, and finished products, and they reflect several aspects of textile production as it was run and supervised by the central authorities of the Mycenaean centres of the southern Greek Mainland and Crete (Killen 2007). A high level of craftsmanship and specialization is conveyed in the documents, indicated by professional designations related to textile production. Among these are the spinner (*a-ra-ka-te-ja*), the weaver (*i-te-ja*), and the seamstress (*ra-pi-ti-ra*), while other terms, usually in the feminine, are more obscure in their meaning (Del Freo et al. 2010). Moreover, the Linear B texts collectively refer to several different, more or less standardized types of textiles or garments (Nosch 2012; Nosch 2014), some of which are described with reference to their colour. A large group of the tablets found at Knossos record the complete cycle of wool production and processing, from the management of sheep (Rougemont 2014) to the allocation of the raw material to textile workers and the delivery of finished items (Killen 2007, 52–53; Nosch 2014). Apart from wool, the only other type of textile fibre identified in the Linear B terminology is flax, in the designation of cloth items as *ri-ta*, linen (Del Freo et al. 2010, 344).

The Linear B texts are the earliest, secure testimony from the Aegean region for a gendered division of textile labour. Women and girls enlisted in the palatial workforce of cloth production outnumber references on men who were most probably involved in the finishing stage of the operational sequence (Killen 2007, 55). The status of these women is not clear, and was probably not homogeneous from one place to the other. At best, however, they were semi-dependent from the central administrations, since the texts testify that they received rations of food from the palatial authorities. The tablets of Pylos hint at the possibility that some of the female workers were captives of war (Killen 2007, 56). The picture emerging from the Mycenaean texts on the organization and specialization of the palatial textile industries should not be considered necessarily representative for non-palatial contexts of production, or for the total chronological span of the Bronze Age.

2.2.6 Experimental Methodologies in Aegean Textiles Research

Experimentation as a research methodology for understanding ancient textile craft has a long tradition in northern Europe, especially in Scandinavia (Olofsson 2015, 25–29, with references). Experimental methods target two main research themes: first, the reconstruction of ancient textile technologies (e.g., Andersson Strand and Nosch 2015; Ulanowska 2016, 325–327; Ulanowska 2018a; Ulanowska 2018b) and second, the reconstruction of garments and other textile items depicted in art iconography or found as textile remains (Jones 2015).

Specialists in Aegean Bronze Age textiles have often included craft experiments and related reconstructions in their studies (Carington Smith 1992, 675, 694, Plates 11.1–11.11; Barber 2016, 205), however systematic employment of the experimental methodology in research projects has so far been pursued at the University of Copenhagen (research project 'Tools and Textiles-Texts and Contexts' at CTR) and at the University of Warsaw. Besides testing the function of spindle whorls and discoid loomweights (Olofsson et al. 2015, 77–78), the CTR experiments included weaving on a warp-weighted loom with the use of copies of crescent-shaped loomweights (Wisti-Lassen 2015) and copies of unpierced clay spools found at Chania, Crete, used as loomweights (Olofsson et al. 2015, 92–95).

A series of systematic experiments with copies of possible textile tools was carried out at the University of Warsaw. One of those targeted exploring the potential loomweight function of unpierced clay spools (Siennicka and Ulanowska 2016). The working hypothesis of the experiment was that, depending on their size, these objects were multi-purpose within the frame of textile craft (bobbins for thread, tablet-weaving weights, loomweights, shuttles, reels used in the warping of the horizontal ground loom, implements for other cloth-producing techniques such as plaiting). Another experiment at the University of Warsaw focused on weaving with the use of the rigid heddle, a simple device for interlacing warp and weft, not identified so far among the material remains of textile tools recovered from the Bronze Age Aegean (but see Nosch and Ulanowska 2021, 92–94, for the interpretation of a sign of the Cretan Hieroglyphic script as a rigid heddle referent). Moreover, the manufacture of clay loomweights similar to those of the Aegean Bronze Age was carried out, as well as weaving on a warp-weighted loom (Ulanowska 2016).

The patterned, often multicoloured, and occasionally figured textiles of the garments depicted on the wall-painting and glyptic art of the second millennium BCE have been the focus of extended discussion on textile motifs and manufacturing techniques (Sapouna-Sakellaraki 1971, 153–195; Barber 1991, 311–382; Tzachili 1997; Jones 2015; Shaw and Chapin 2016; Peterson Murray 2016; Sarri 2024). Experimental weaving has been employed to recreate textile patterns similar to those represented in Aegean Bronze Age art and to explore alternative hypotheses on the techniques, the tools and the skill required for pattern-weaving (e.g., Barber 1991, 325–326; Spantidaki 2008; Ulanowska 2018a).

Experimental reconstruction of complete dresses is exemplified in the work of Bernice Jones (2015, with references). In her work, Jones stresses the importance of observing details on the artistic representation of dress, to understand the design and the sartorial choices that would have ultimately shaped the various types of Aegean garments.

3 Weaving the Threads of Aegean Bronze Age Textile Histories

This section weaves together the results of studies on textile tools, production facilities, and excavated textiles of the Bronze Age Aegean. It is structured around a basic chronological framework, following the conventional division into the Early, Middle, and Late Bronze Age – the latter further subdivided into an early and a late phase. Within each chronological period, the material is organized geographically into three main regions: Crete, the (remainder of the) insular region, and the Greek Mainland. Each regional section is then divided into two parts, according to the main categories of archaeological evidence: (a) textile tools and production facilities, and (b) excavated textiles and imprints. This regional and categorical structure is not rigidly repeated within every chronological section. Instead, the narrative flows from one region or category to another, guided by content-based considerations – such as the availability of evidence and the extent to which earlier discussions inform subsequent ones. For instance, the Early Bronze Age section begins with the insular region, where the earliest imprints of Aegean woven textiles were testified in Final Neolithic to Early Cycladic I contexts on the islands of Kea and Astypalaia respectively. The Middle Bronze Age section, however, begins with Crete because its textile-related archaeological record provides the background to understand the textile craft of the second millennium BCE in the Aegean region as a whole.

3.1 The Early Bronze Age

3.1.1 The Insular Region

Excavated Textiles and Imprints

By the beginning of the EBA, finely woven textiles were used in the Aegean region. Evidence for this exists in the form of a few textile imprints, like those on the soil that was filling the clay vessel used for an infant inhumation, found at Vathy, Astypalaia (Vlachopoulos 2024, 667–674, Figs. 11–12), and in the walls of pottery sherds found at Kephala on Kea, presumably created during the manufacture of the respective pots (Carington Smith 1977), dated as early as the Final Neolithic period. It is clear, therefore, that the textile craft practiced at the dawn of the third millennium BCE did not emerge in a vacuum but was drawing from the achievements and traditions of centuries-old technologies.

Several centuries of cloth production intervene between the Kea imprints and the next direct textile evidence from the insular Aegean (Table 1, Table 2). At the Early Cycladic (EC) II cemetery of Dokathismata, on the island of Amorgos, one of the graves included a bronze dagger (Figure 12) that preserved the mineralized fragment of a textile on its surface (Gavalas 2018, 182). The fragment appears to have belonged to a finely woven cloth. Although described as linen in the literature (Gavalas 2018, 182; Barber 1991, 174, n.12), no fibre analysis for this textile has been published to date.

More evidence of cloth from EC Amorgos, in the form of textile imprints, emerged from the excavation of Markiani, a settlement on a rocky slope that was founded in the early third millennium BCE (Marangou et al. 2006). Three pottery sherds from the site manifest imprints of woven structures that were identified as cloth (Renfrew 2006, 199, Fig. 8.18, Plate 45). All three show plain

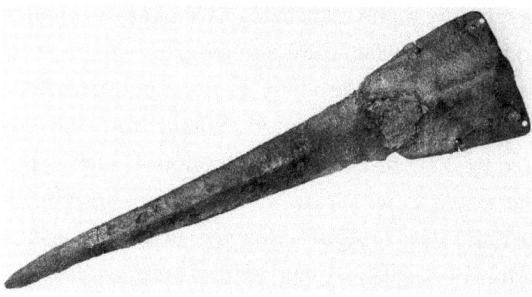

Figure 12 Bronze dagger with mineralized textile fragment from Dokathismata, Amorgos, Cyclades (inv. nr. 4720 © Hellenic National Archaeological Museum/ODAP/Hellenic Ministry of Culture).

weaves. The contexts of these sherds were dated to Markiani phases III and IV (EC II early and late phases respectively) (Renfrew et al. 2006).

Another case of woven cloth impressed on a malleable surface derives from Akrotiri, Thera. A cylinder of reddish-orange pigment was found in an EC context and thus quite probably dates from the third millennium BCE (Birtacha et al. 2021). Its surface preserves the imprint of a woven structure and a rectangular stamp impression. The cloth imprint reflects plain weave and is described as 'fine and coarse' so at least two qualities of fabric are attested (Birtacha et al. 2021, Fig. 2). Another example from Akrotiri derives from a special context known as the 'Sacrificial Complex', found along with a concentration of EC artefacts (Doumas 2008, 165–166) and thus considered as an EC assemblage. This is a metal tool that has preserved the fragment of a cloth in mineralized state on its surface (Papadima 2005, 81). Moreover, remains of a textile were traced on a metal pin dated to the EC period (Michaelidis and Angelidis 2006, 69).

Textile Tools and Production Facilities

Textile tools dated to the beginning of the EBA are documented at the site of Poliochni on Lemnos. Large numbers of clay, well-shaped, often burnished but undecorated, biconical, and conical spindle whorls were found in deposits of the Blue period (Bernabò Brea 1964, 155) corresponding to the EB I horizon. The excavator also reported cylindrical, clay objects with one longitudinal perforation from the same period which, if interpreted as loomweights, may indicate the use of the warp-weighted loom (Bernabò Brea 1964, 658). Such cylindrical clay objects were also found at a contemporary site on the island of Thasos, in the north Aegean. A small settlement radiocarbon-dated to the early EBA was excavated at the bay of Ayios Ioannis, on the southeast coast of the island (Papadopoulos et al. 2018, 361–363). Nine perforated cylinders, manufactured

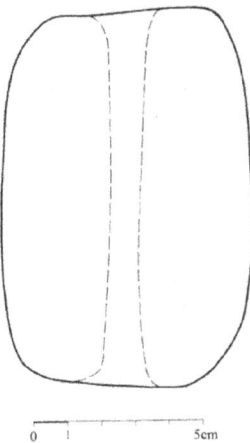

Figure 13 Cylindrical loomweight with one perforation from Ayios Ioannis, Thasos (drawing by S. Vakirtzi).

in large sizes and weighing between 500 and 1000 gr, were found and have been identified as loomweights (Figure 13). Their thickness, ranging between 6 and 9 cm, likely suggests very open or weft-faced weaves, while their weight requires thick threads. The over thirty spindle whorls found at the site confirm local production of medium to thick threads: shaped predominantly in the discoid-lentoid type, the majority of the whorls weigh between 30 and 60 gr (Papadopoulos et al. 2018, 361–363; Vakirtzi 2018a). If Carington Smith was right in suggesting that cylindrical loomweights would have been used in sets of eight to ten (1975, 219), then the assemblage of Ayios Ioannis likely corresponds to a more or less complete weaving set for one loom.

In the Cyclades, textile craft of the EC I period is documented through conical spindle whorls that are reported from the EC I sites of Avyssos and Pyrgos on the island of Paros (Rambach 2000, 196–197). At the settlement of Skarkos on the island of Ios, a few contexts attributed to the EC I period (Marthari 2017; Maniatis et al. 2023) yielded c. twenty clay spindle whorls that are noteworthy for their typological homogeneity. These are predominantly low conical spindle whorls, while just a few are discoid (Vakirtzi 2018a; Vakirtzi 2020). More than half of the overall whorl assemblage includes heavy tools, reaching up to 70 gr, indicating spinning (or plying) thick thread, as in EB I Thasos (Vakirtzi 2020).

During the EB II period, spindle whorls were manufactured and used in settlements spanning from the north Aegean (Skala Sotiros, Thasos), to the Eastern Aegean islands (Poliochni and Koukonisi on Lemnos, Emporio on Chios, Thermi on Lesbos) to the south (Heraion on Samos) clearly indicating the importance of yarn production in the respective communities (Vakirtzi 2020, with references). In the Cyclades, thread spinning or plying is attested in settlements including Ayia Irini on Kea (Wilson 1999), Markiani on Amorgos (Gavalas 2018) Dhaskalio (Gavalas 2013) and Skarkos on Ios where the spindle whorl assemblage now includes biconical and cylindrical types of whorls in addition to the low conical type of the preceding period (Vakirtzi 2018a).

The spindle whorl assemblages of Ayia Irini, Markiani, and Skarkos demonstrate that thread production was not particularly standardized, as suggested by the range of whorl sizes comprising each assemblage. However, they all include tools that are lighter than 20 gr while the heaviest ones have a less pronounced representation (Vakirtzi 2015; Gavalas 2018; Vakirtzi 2020). This indicates a subtle shift in comparison to the EC/EB I period, with finer rather than coarse thread production at the core of the yarn industries. Among the smallest spindle whorls are those weighing up to 15 gr, found at Skala Sotiros on Thasos, Heraion on Samos, Ayia Irini on Keos, and Koukonisi on Lemnos (Vakirtzi 2018a; Vakirtzi 2020).

Another aspect of thread manufacture in EBA insular societies is highlighted by the fact that tools have sometimes been found in graves (Vakirtzi 2018b). It is noteworthy that some very small, clay whorls weighing between 3 and 10 gr were deposited as burial offerings in a grave at the EC cemetery of Aplomata on Naxos (Vakirtzi 2018b; Vakirtzi 2020). Tools of this size class can be used to produce extremely thin woollen and linen threads that can be then woven into cloth, as the CTR spinning experiments performed with wool and flax show (Möller-Wiering 2015, 103–109). Metal needles that are part of the EC material culture, and were also deposited in tombs as burial offerings (Doumas 1977, 60; Rambach 2000, 172–173), occasionally in the same tomb with spindle whorls (Rambach 2000, Tafel 63), indicate sewing or embroidery. The smallest and lightest EBA whorls imply careful preparation of the fibres before the spinning stage, a process that requires a considerable amount of time (Andersson Strand 2015). Could the custom of depositing textile tools in graves provide insights to the gender of the islanders who spun thread and sewed? Unfortunately, preserved skeletal remains from the EBA Aegean are minimal. This does not allow us to reach any conclusions on the biological sex, let alone the gender of the people who were buried with spindles and whorls (Vakirtzi 2018b).

Distribution patterns of textile tools in the insular settlements indicate household production. Spinning toolkits that can be ascribed to a single household or production area usually include whorls of considerably different sizes, indicating a tendency to address the need for at least two distinct qualities of thread. Such a nuanced picture is provided by the excavator of the prehistoric settlement at the Heraion on the island of Samos, dated in the late third millennium BCE (Milojčić 1961). In one case, a group of five spindle whorls was traced in the east part of the 'Großes Haus', and in a second case, a group of six spindle whorls was found in a clay vessel in the 'Magazine' building (Milojčić 1961, 23–24, 51). When a sample of these tools was studied, it became clear that each of these small concentrations included spindle whorls of significantly different sizes, from very small to large (Vakirtzi 2018a, 192) (Supplementary Figure 6). A preliminary distribution study of the tools found at Skarkos on Ios reveals a similar picture (Vakirtzi 2018a, 193).

During the EB II period, a spindle whorl type with a hollow top (a concave configuration around the central perforation also known as 'scodelletta'), often decorated with incised, geometric motifs, was used in the northeastern Aegean islands of Lemnos (Figure 14), Lesbos and Chios (Barber 1991, 306–307; Vakirtzi 2020). Examples of this type of whorl were also found in the Cyclades, at Dhaskalio and Markiani (Gavalas 2018), and in EC II cemeteries on Syros (Chalandriani) and Naxos (Aplomata) (Vakirtzi 2020). To date, however, no such whorls have been found at Skarkos on Ios, while they are rather rare in the EC II–III deposits of Ayia Irini on Kea (Wilson 1999). Barber (1991) surveyed parallels of this type of tool found in earlier sites, from central Asia and Anatolia, and in later sites in northern Italy and as far as Switzerland. She distinguished a gradual, centuries-long westward diffusion of the 'scodelletta' spindle whorl type, which she attributed to population mobility (Barber 1991, 299–310).

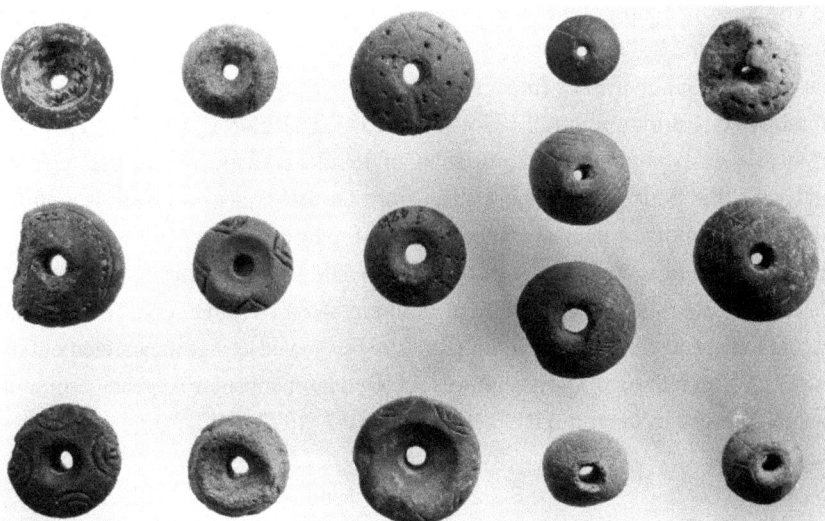

Figure 14 Spindle whorls of the decorated, 'scodelletta' type from Poliochni, Lemnos (Bernabò Brea 1976, Vol. II.2, Tav. CCXXXI, ©Archivi SAIA, C/18905).

Weaving on the warp-weighted loom in the EBA Aegean is indicated at a few insular sites of the northeast Aegean. One of those is Poliochni on Lemnos, where cylindrical weights are reported from the horizon of the Green and Red towns (EB II early) (Bernabò Brea 1964, 658, Pl. CLXVII: 9). Another one is Thermi on Lesbos, where discoid loomweights have been found (Carington Smith 1975, 237). At Ayia Irini on Kea, in the Cyclades, weaving with the technology of the warp-weighted loom is also demonstrated through the recovery of clay loomweights (Wilson 1999, 160) that have been described as 'Anatolian type' tools (Davis 1984, 162). Stone weights of similar shape and size found in the same location, indeed in the same deposits (Davis 1984, 154–155), were probably also used as loomweights. It is possible that three similar stone weights found at the EC II-late site of Panormos on Naxos (Devetzi 2014, 338–340), had had a loomweight use as well. These finds indicate the possible use of the warp-weighted loom in the Cyclades during the third millennium BCE, perhaps using stone loomweights. However, the most exhaustively excavated EC settlements to date, namely Markiani on Amorgos, Dhaskalio near Keros and Skarkos on Ios, did not yield either clay or stone loomweights of this type or any other identifiable type (Gavalas 2018; Marthari 2018, 189–192). It is possible that in these settlements either warp-weighted looms were operated with weights made of perishable materials that have not survived in the archaeological deposits; or that loom types other than the warp-weighted were used, like the horizontal ground looms or other weaving devices.

The anatolianizing element identified in the loomweight types of Ayia Irini, Kea, and in the hollow, incised whorls of several insular settlements, with clear parallels in Anatolian sites (most notably in Troy, Balfanz 1995) have long been highlighted (Carington Smith 1975; Davis 1984, 162; Barber 1991). These types of textile tools suggest the integration of textile craftspeople in the regional networks that flourished in the Aegean from the EB II period onwards, and the nodal position of the insular communities in the trajectories that brought people into contact. Finished products of the loom would also have circulated from one place to another, at least as items of clothing worn by travellers. Textile craft, textile tools, and cloth items should therefore be viewed as significant elements of the EBA 'International Spirit' that was fostered by the insular Aegean communities in the third millennium BCE (Renfrew 2017 [1972]).

3.1.2 The Mainland

Excavated Textile Imprints

A small, clay sealing found at Geraki, Laconia, in the southern Peloponnese, preserves the imprint of finely woven cloth (Weingarten 2000). The context is dated to the EH IIB period, a time of increased connectivity in the Aegean. The imprint demonstrates a plain, faced weave structure (Table 2). Vogelsang-Eastwood (1999) identified a possible selvedge and perhaps the starting border of the cloth, a feature indicating weaving on a warp-weighted loom. She also highlighted a structure identified as the interlacing of warps and wefts in one location, where 'the crossing of several threads in both systems 1 and 2' were observed (Vogelsang-Eastwood 1999, 372–373, Fig. 21). This find indicates the use of fine textiles in activities such as the sealing practices that resulted in the creation of the Geraki imprint (Weingarten 2000). The sealings of Geraki were most probably created within the Peloponnese, and perhaps even at the site itself (Weingarten et al. 1999, 368–370), so the cloth too was available in the location where the sealing process took place. Nonetheless, it is unknown where, or by whom, this finely woven textile was produced.

Textile Tools and Production Facilities

Textile craft in the EBA across the Greek Mainland is documented by spindle whorls and loomweights found at various sites. This material, first surveyed by Carington Smith (1975, 196–260, passim), confirms that thread manufacture with spindle and whorl and weaving on the warp-weighted loom were widespread textile technologies. Their morphometric variability indicates diverse production targets, relating to both thread qualities and cloth types, observed across different sites as well as within each site. The general impression is one of accentuated regionality. Within this technological mosaic, Carington Smith has emphasized the hemispherical whorl and the cylindrical loomweight as the most commonly found tool types in the region (Smith 1975, 219). Besides these, the pyramidal and the spherical loomweight types also occur, while other types are rare (Smith 1975, 237–260).

In the Peloponnese, textile craft of this period is well documented in the Argolid. Spindle whorls are very common finds, but loomweights are few and have been found scattered in archaeological deposits, often as isolated items (Siennicka 2020). This distribution can be hardly representative of weaving sets and can only be indicative of the use of the warp-weighted loom, perhaps at a small scale. At Lerna, large numbers of spindle whorls have been found (Banks 1967), chronologically distributed across two main phases, EH II and EH III (Siennicka 2023), separated by important changes at the site (Pullen 2008, 36, 39). Thread manufacture was practiced throughout the settlement's life, although the types and sizes of tools differ slightly from one phase to the other. The comparison of the whorl assemblages of the two phases indicates changes in the ways the tools were modelled, perhaps due to a shift in the average quality of the fibres (Banks 1967, 538; Siennicka 2023): the EH II assemblage is highly standardized, composed of hemispherical (or 'domed') clay whorls with plain, undecorated surfaces. This standardization recedes in EH III, when conical and biconical types are used along with hemispherical ones. Moreover, decorated, incised whorls like those observed in the islands, are now noted here, too, considered by Banks as 'almost certainly not locally made' (Banks 1967, 537). The size range in the whorl groups of both chronological phases is wide, but most of the EH II whorls were manufactured in large, heavy sizes implying a focus on the production of thick threads, while lighter specimens appear to have increased in the next phase (Siennicka 2020; Siennicka 2023, 148–150). Siennicka interprets the typological and metrological shift as potentially indicating a shift in textile fibre from bast to wool (Siennicka 2023, 148–150), while a similar pattern was observed at the EH I–II site of Tsoungiza in Corinthia (Siennicka 2023, 150–151).

Weaving at Lerna is less clearly documented, with only a few loomweights found in EH deposits: Banks recorded just five from periods III and IV (EH II–III), manufactured in the 'parallelepiped' (with two longitudinal or lengthwise perforations) and the cylindrical (with either one or two longitudinal perforations) types (Banks 1967, 565–566). Siennicka (2020, 34) highlights the occurrence of a cylindrical and a 'parallelepiped' loomweight on the floor of a room along with one spindle whorl, underlining that the latter loomweight was stamped several times with a seal. A few clay spools, that might have been used in textile production as loomweights, were also found at Lerna, marking the transition from the EH III period to the MH I. The third millennium BCE examples are less than ten, including pierced and unpierced items, all from EH III deposits (Banks 1967, 551–560).

The hemispherical whorl type is also noted at other EH sites in northeastern Peloponnese, including Korakou and Zygouries (Carington Smith 1975, 199) as well as in EH deposits at Tiryns (Rahmstorf et al. 2015, 269). Siennicka (2023) has argued that this regional typological homogeneity (Figure 15),

Figure 15 Hemispherical spindle whorls from Tiryns, Argolid (image reproduced from Siennicka 2023 ©M. Siennicka).

Figure 16 Crescent-shaped loomweight from Tiryns, Argolid (image courtesy of M. Siennicka ©M. Siennicka).

along with the good firing and surface treatment, likely suggest that in this area spindle whorl manufacture might have been carried out in specialized pottery workshops (Siennicka 2020, 28). Moreover, she has observed that this is in sharp contrast to the manufacture of weaving implements, considering, for example, the cylinders with three perforations found at Tiryns, which were carelessly made of coarse clay and were left unfired or half-baked (Siennicka 2020, 28). Another type of loomweight attested at EH Tiryns is the crescent-shaped, with two perforations, each near one distal end (Rahmstorf et al. 2015) (Figure 16). This weaving implement reveals an Anatolian influence, and is considered suitable for producing diagonal (or twill) weave (Wisti-Lassen 2015). This loomweight type was also attested in EH deposits at Geraki, Laconia (Crouwel et al. 2007), where the textile imprint discussed earlier was found. Twill weave, however, has not yet been documented in cloth form in the Aegean Bronze Age, even though it had been used in matting since the Neolithic (Perlès 2001, 243).

In northern Greece, textile production was documented in domestic units at a settlement excavated near Archontiko, Giannitsa, dated to the late third millennium BCE (Papadopoulou et al. 2015). The excavators have reported that the spinning equipment, consisting of large, clay spindle whorls in various types, reflects the production of thick threads. The weavers were using pyramidal loomweights, in a range of sizes, from light to very heavy, and with thicknesses that are compatible with open or faced textiles (Papadopoulou et al. 2015, 294–295). A similar picture emerges from EBA Sitagroi, where (mostly biconical) spindle whorls in various sizes, and loomweights of both cylindrical and pyramidal type, were found in domestic contexts (Elster 2003). A varied textile production has been speculated, most probably with a focus on thick threads and coarse textiles in plain balanced weave (Elster et al. 2015).

On present evidence, the textile production across Mainland Greece during the course of the third millennium BCE appears diversified possibly with a focus on coarser products, though not excluding the manufacture of fine threads and finely woven textiles. Fine thread production, suggested by small and light spindle whorls, points to a thorough preparation of textile fibres prior to spinning or splicing. This entails some degree of specialization, as fibre processing is quite time-consuming (Andersson Strand 2015a). Where contextual data is available, it indicates that the production of cloth was organized at the household level, but there is no evidence regarding the division of textile labour, for example along gender lines.

3.1.3 Crete

Textile Tools and Production Facilities

No fragments of cloth or textile imprints dated to the third millennium BCE have been published from Crete to date. Nevertheless, the preservation of textile tools and the identification of spaces for textile processing (Burke 2010, 26–31), allow some hypotheses on EM textile production. From the loomweight evidence alone, the technology of the warp-weighted loom in EM Crete appears to have been quite widespread in the central and eastern part of the island. However, at some EM sites textile craft is indicated only by spindle whorls (Cutler 2021, 62), leaving open the possibility that other types of looms were used as well. Nonetheless, with regard to the warp-weighted loom, the typological variability of loomweights across the central/east region is noteworthy: as Burke (Burke 2010) and Cutler (2021, 61–62) point out, textile tools found in EM II deposits at Knossos, Myrtos, and Vasiliki include cylindrical, discoid, spherical and, in the case of the latter site, cuboid loomweights (Cutler 2021, 61). Knossos yielded a few domed and cylindrical loomweights from EM II contexts, and by the MM IA phase, the earliest examples of what would later become the hallmark of Knossian Protopalatial weaving, the discoid loomweight type, appear (Figure 11, f–g). The best representation of EM discoid loomweights to date are published from the settlement of Myrtos, on the south coast of Crete (Warren 1972). Those were found along with a group of pierced stones, also interpreted as possible loomweights (Poursat 2012). At Phaistos, the remains of an EM settlement explored beneath the palatial complex did not yield securely identified loomweights. However, spindle whorls, mostly heavy hemispherical ones reaching up to 100 gr in weight, small and light cylindrical ones, and biconical ones that came in both small and large sizes, indicate a variable thread production (Militello 2014a, 252–253). The Phaistos whorls are well manufactured and have a careful surface finish (Militello 2014a, 252–253) but, unlike Myrtos, no painted examples were found among them (Warren 1972, 262–263; Burke 2010, 27). At Myrtos, thread making is also testified on

Figure 17 Spinning bowl from Myrtos, Crete (image reproduced from Warren 1972, Pl. 68, image courtesy of ©P. Warren).

the basis of clay spinning bowls (Figure 17), believed to have been used for plying thread. As Burke notes, these are among the earliest examples of spinning bowls found in the Eastern Mediterranean, making it likely that this textile implement and the related plying technique were Cretan inventions (Burke 2010, 29). Zavadil recently raised awareness as to the lack of use wear traces in vessels of this type found in Western Peloponnese, in contrast to the Cretan examples, thus their use for textile production in the Peloponnese was questioned (Zavadil 2023).

Overall, the technological landscape of textile craft in EM Crete is characterized by regionalism. This variability indicates different types of textiles woven by different communities. Most of this evidence is found in the eastern part of the island, as the Early Minoan is not well documented in west Crete (Cutler 2021, 62). Where there is good contextual data, textile production appears organized at the household level (Burke 2010). The contextual association of loomweights with built structures and installations interpreted as basins, drains, and vats at Myrtos, combined with the results of organic residue analysis that identified animal lipids in one of these features, led Warren to argue that wool washing and probably wool dyeing took place in the settlement (Warren 1972). The suggestion that wool was an important textile fibre finds further, indirect support in the emergence of dye workshops in the same region, at least as early as EM III (Brogan et al. 2012). This would be in agreement with dress iconography: as discussed in Section 2.2.1, some of the anthropomorphic vessels dating from EM II to EM III, indicate sophisticated sartorial choices, patterned cloth and quite possibly multicoloured textiles (see also Stefani 2013).

3.2 The Middle Bronze Age

3.2.1 Protopalatial Crete

Excavated Textiles

Direct textile evidence from Protopalatial Crete is very limited. Small, calcified cloth fragments found at Malia (Figure 18) were identified and collected during the examination of water flotation residue, conducted as part of an archaeobotanical study (Sarpaki 2007, 884). Their deposit derived from a drain on the east edge of Quartier Mu, a large building complex that hosted weaving activities at several locations (Cutler 2021, 123–131) before its destruction in MM IIB. After examination of one of the fragments, Cutler et al. (2013) diagnosed a plain, balanced weave (Table 2). They also distinguished different threads used for the two thread systems, spun in opposite directions (*s* and *z* respectively). Based on the z-twist direction of the one thread system, they proposed that the textile was woven partly of woollen yarn (Cutler et al. 2013, 118). No further analysis of this textile fragment for fibre identification has been published to date, leaving open the possibility that this may be the earliest documentation of wool in the Aegean, slightly predating the woollen, carbonized threads of Akrotiri, Thera (see Section 3.3.2).

Textile Tools and Production Facilities

In the Protopalatial period major weaving centres emerged across Crete, established within or around the first palaces, while textile production is also

Figure 18 Calcified cloth fragments from Malia, Crete
(image courtesy of ©A. Sarpaki).

documented in contemporary urban centres. Overall, the weaving stage is well documented owing to loomweights. However, one of the most puzzling aspects of Protopalatial textile industries concerns the low archaeological visibility of thread manufacture (Burke 2010, 50). The pattern of scarcity of spindle whorls on Bronze Age Crete observed in early research (Carington Smith 1975, 261, 266) appears to persist, at least with regard to the large weaving centres. If threads were manufactured with the spinning technique, necessitating spindles equipped with whorls, then the scarcity of whorls at the Protopalatial centres demonstrates that spinning was marginal and performed at a limited scale (Cutler 2021, passim). The hypothesis of an alternative technique of thread making, namely splicing, cannot satisfactorily explain this scarcity, since it requires plying the spliced threads with a spindle and whorl, as well (Gleba and Harris 2019, 2333, 2341). Nonetheless, splicing may be indicated by the occurrence of spinning bowls at a number of Protopalatial sites, in a technical tradition that continued from the Prepalatial period (Burke 2010, 19, 61; Militello 2014a, 135–138). Other hypotheses have also been proposed, for example, that the spindles and whorls might have been primarily wooden, like the Egyptian ones, and therefore would not have survived in the archaeological record, or that spinning would have taken place at locations other than the major sites (Burke 2010, 50). The clay spindle whorls recovered from small settlements in the periphery of the large centres support the latter scenario.

The typological repertoire and the metric data of textile tools from Protopalatial sites have been published in a systematic way in recent publications (e.g., Burke 2003; Militello 2014a; Cutler 2016b) but in older works they are often very briefly mentioned, without their weight or diameter values. From what can be surmised based on the most comprehensive reports, spindle whorl sizes fluctuate from 10 gr to more than 80 gr (Cutler 2021, 74, 111, 131). Thus, a pattern of a diversified thread manufacture emerges from this period as well. This corresponds well with the most striking feature of Protopalatial weaving, the wide variety of loomweights, both in terms of types and sizes (Cutler 2021): the typological repertoire across Crete includes discoid, spherical, cuboid, cylindrical, rectangular, torus-shaped, and truncated- pyramidal tools made of clay, as well as pierced stone pebbles, in a range of sizes (Cutler 2021, passim). Some weaving centres manifest only one type, for example the Protopalatial weaving workshop at Knossos, which relied exclusively on discoid loomweights (Cutler 2021, 70–71). Most of the other locations, however, yielded assemblages consisting of various, different types. The dominant loomweight type differs from one place to the other: unlike Knossos, Phaistos lacks discoid loomweights and instead documents cylindrical ones in this period (Militello 2014a, 253–254; Cutler 2021, 109). At Malia various types were used, and probably pierced pebbles as well, with a noted predominance of the spherical type (Cutler 2021, 123–131). At Petras in East Crete cuboid loomweights were found in secure Protopalatial deposits, while in the town of Palaikastro, some fills dated to the Protopalatial period included discoid, cuboid, spherical, and pyramidal types (Cutler 2021, 154). The weight and thickness ranges of the loomweights in these deposits differ considerably (Cutler 2021, passim), demonstrating a functional variability. Generally, discoid loomweights were used to weave dense fabrics with fine threads, while spherical and cylindrical ones were suitable for open weaves or weft-faced textiles. Thus, although the warp-weighted loom was widely employed for weaving across the island, this technological choice did not preclude a rich variety of woven products. Protopalatial Cretan weaving was not homogeneous across the island.

However, at Knossos textile production appears to have been highly standardized. Although a few spherical loomweights, along with discoid ones, were found in Protopalatial deposits in the Royal Road South, an area outside of the Palace (Cutler 2021, 73), at the palatial complex itself a large assemblage of about four hundred discoid loomweights was found in an area designated as 'the Loomweight Basement' (Cutler 2021, 70–72). It consists of very standardized tools in shape and size: after examining a sample of these, Cutler recorded a thickness range between 1.5 cm and 2.5 cm and a weight range between 128 gr and 200 gr (Cutler 2021, 71, Fig. 6.17). This is a group of tools that points to the manufacture of very fine, densely woven, plain, balanced cloth.

Protopalatial Malia has yielded one of the largest corpora of loomweights on Crete. Weavers based at this palatial centre were using a wide range of loomweights (Cutler 2021, 123–131) but the most frequently attested is the spherical, with discoid ones being much less reported. Thus, textile production at Malia likely differed considerably from that of Knossos. Spherical weights were often found in the same buildings either alongside pierced pebbles or with other types of clay loomweights (Poursat 2013, Pl. 46i) (Figure 19), so that a range of textiles would have been produced even within the same building/weaving workshop. Malia is one of the earliest Cretan sites to demonstrate the use of spherical loomweights, a type that later became dominant in Knossos and at other weaving centres of the Neopalatial period. It should be noted that the excavation at Malia also yielded pointed bone implements known as 'pin beaters' (Poursat 1996, Pl. 44a) (Figure 20). These tools have been interpreted as specialized implements used in tapestry weaving in the Eastern Mediterranean (Smith 2013). The preference for spherical loomweights, suitable to produce open or weft-faced fabrics is compatible with pattern weaving (Cutler 2021, 249–251), in an arrangement where wefts perhaps even multicoloured ones, would be packed against the more openly arranged warps, to create the desired motifs.

Clothing Bodies 39

Figure 19 Group of spherical and cylindrical loomweights in situ, from Quartier Mu, Malia, Crete (image reproduced from Poursat 2013, Pl. 46i ©École Française d'Athènes/Jean Claude Poursat, Negative Nr. L1932-026A).

Figure 20 Bone implements known as 'pin beaters' from Malia, Crete (image reproduced from Poursat 1996, Pl. 44a ©École Française d'Athènes/Émile Sérafis, Negative Nr. 35068).

The production of multicoloured textiles in Protopalatial Crete is suggested by an additional category of archaeological finds. Facilities and debris of dye workshops have been identified in the late EM period (Brogan et al. 2012, 187), while the production of dyes probably intensified in the early second millennium BCE (Burke 2010, 34–39). Archaeological finds such as piles of crushed murex shells, basins, hearths and pounding tools, concentrating mostly in Eastern Crete, suggest the production of purple dye (Brogan et al. 2012). A configuration of basins and vats on the bedrock at the site of Alatzomouri-Pefka in East Crete revealed an important workshop for the manufacture of more than one dye (Apostolakou et al. 2020). Organic residue analysis on ceramic utensils indicated that along with purple from the murex shell, yellow and red colours from vegetal resources such as weld and madder were also being produced there (Koh et al. 2016). The flourishing of purple and other dye industries potentially indicates the rising importance of wool economy during this period, since dyes are better absorbed by wool.[3]

The hundreds of loomweights of various types, the weaving locations, the dye workshops, and even the few scraps of mineralized Protopalatial cloth found to date, create the impression of a dynamic textile landscape, reflected also in the textile imagery of this period, with the first clear depictions of patterned textiles used for garments, as discussed in Section 2.2.1 (Sapouna-Sakellaraki 1971, 7–29; Barber 1991, 314; Stefani 2013, 55–79; Jones 2015, 25–55 esp. 36). Pattern weaving with multicoloured woollen wefts was probably one of the key technical achievements of Protopalatial textile craft. Such elaborately woven textile items (Alberti 2012, 126–127) were desired by the elites in kingdoms located beyond the Aegean as far as Mari, and were either delivered there, or locally crafted by Near Eastern (or travelling Aegean?) weavers in 'the Cretan style', according to the Mariote palace's cuneiform archives dating to the eighteenth century BCE (Aruz 2008, 117; Alberti 2012).

3.2.2 The Insular Region

Textile fragments contemporaneous with the Protopalatial period of Crete have not been published to date from the Cyclades, the northern Aegean, the southeastern or the southwestern Aegean. Textile consumption is very poorly known, owing not only to the lack of excavated textiles, but also due to a lack of iconographic evidence for clothing, with very few exceptions (see Section 2.2.1).

The most significant body of work on weaving craft in the island communities of the early second millennium BCE was carried out by J. Cutler (2021) who

---

[3] Note, however, that purple dye was identified in a group of textiles found in Grave Circle A, Mycenae, whose primary material was preliminarily reported as flax (Spantidaki 2022).

systematically analysed extensive loomweight assemblages and compared them to the archaeological record of Crete. Thus, she was able to contrast the varied technological landscape of weaving on Protopalatial Crete, that defies the monolithic term 'Minoan', to a much more standardized production on the Aegean islands during the MBA, where weaving on the warp-weighted loom appears to have specialized in a certain type of cloth, attainable with the use of the discoid loomweights of Cretan type.

At present, the earliest contact points between the Cretan weaving technology and the Aegean archipelago, manifest in the discoid loomweights, are documented at MBA Kolonna on Aegina (Cutler 2021, 241) and at MC Akrotiri, Thera, where three, extremely standardized, discoid loomweights were found in Phase A deposits equivalent to the transitional EC III/MC I phase (Vakirtzi 2019) (Figure 21). Significantly, the Akrotiri examples are manufactured of apparently local, Theran clay, suggesting that these particular loomweights had not been transported from Crete. It must be emphasized that weaving on the warp-weighted loom on the islands in the beginning of the MBA testifies, not generally a Cretan, but specifically a Knossian influence, where the discoid was the dominant loomweight type.

In the early MBA insular contexts, these tools are very few, usually found in secondary deposits that do not allow for a clear picture of the organization and scale of production. At Ayia Irini on Kea the earliest discoid loomweights date from period IV while at Phylakopi on Melos, from period C (late MBA) (Cutler

Figure 21 Piriform discoid loomweight with one perforation from MC Phase A, from Akrotiri, Thera (photo S. Vakirtzi).

2021, 169–182, 216; Cutler et al. 2024). On Rhodes, in the Dodecanese, Cretan-type loomweights were found in the MBA horizon of the settlement on Mount Philerimos, the port of Akandia, and the town of Trianda (Marketou 2009). By the end of the MBA discoid loomweights were also used at Koukonisi, Lemnos, at Kastri on Kythera and other insular and coastal sites around the Aegean Sea (Cutler 2021, 236, 238).

The use of the horizontal loom in the Cyclades during this period has been suggested in two cases. At Ayia Irini on Kea, and Phylakopi on Melos, a special category of objects, namely pierced clay spools with flaring shafts (Cutler 2021, 169, 215) (Figure 22) may have been used as accessories for reeling the warp threads to prepare them for the horizontal loom (Carington Smith 1975, 404). Ayia Irini yielded more than one hundred spools but only around thirty from secure MC deposits (Cutler 2021, 172, 180) while at Phylakopi, where the Middle Bronze Age horizon was less extensively excavated, twenty-seven spools were recorded (Cutler 2021, 216; Cutler et al. 2024). These objects are more frequently found in Middle Helladic deposits on the southern Greek Mainland (Pavúk 2012) so their occurrence in the Cyclades testifies some degree of technological sharing between the craft communities of the two regions. Moreover, it indicates that the islands could be the 'meeting points' of different technological traditions: along with pierced clay spools with flaring shafts, both Ayia Irini and Phylakopi were employing the technology of the warp-weighted loom at this time, judging by the discoid loomweights found in deposits of the MC horizon.

The selective choice and combination of different traditions by the islanders has one more manifestation. The overwhelming influence of Crete, and more specifically Knossos, over weaving practices and loomweight manufacture in the MC/MBA archipelago, does not seem to have hindered the islanders' use of

Figure 22 Clay spool with flaring shaft, from Ayia Irini, Keos (©Department of Classics University of Cincinnati).

whorls modelled in characteristically insular EBA types, that appear to have been largely absent in EM Crete (Burke 2010, 25–29, with references), such as the hollow, incised ('scodelletta') whorl. It should be recalled that yarn manufacture is practically undocumented at Protopalatial Knossos (Cutler 2021, 74). This is an interesting asymmetry, given the technological, operational, and organizational associations between the spinning and the weaving stages of textile production.

Spindle whorls found at MC Ayia Irini, Phylakopi, and Akrotiri, as well as at MBA Koukonisi, demonstrate that spinning with spindle and whorl was a persistent and widespread thread-making technology (Vakirtzi 2015). However, subtle differences compared to the EBA patterns have been observed. Unlike a more pronounced typological variability across the EBA insular Aegean, in the MC/MBA period the biconical spindle whorl dominates over all other types. This is a whorl type that demonstrates a wide range of sizes, therefore suitable for the manufacture of several different thread qualities (Vakirtzi 2015). Moreover, the use of hollow, incised whorls continues to be manifest in the insular communities where it is well represented, especially at Ayia Irini on Kea (Overbeck 1989; Vakirtzi 2015) and at MBA Koukonisi (Vakirtzi 2015). A metrological analysis on a sample of whorls from MC Ayia Irini, Phylakopi, Akrotiri, and Koukonisi has indicated a pattern of diverse sizes in the toolkits of these settlements, but also revealed a preference for relatively smaller tools in comparison to the earlier period (Vakirtzi 2015). This points to a focus on the production of fine threads that would be compatible with the discoid type of loomweights, considered suitable for weaving fine yarn.

In her discussion of the process of adoption of Cretan weaving technology by communities beyond Crete, Cutler critically examined older theories (Cutler 2021, 248–256) and stressed the varied timing of its initial appearance. This chronological pattern is an indication that in some cases the warp-weighted loom of the Cretan type may have been adopted gradually from one intermediary community to the other, and not directly from Crete (Cutler 2021, 252). As Cutler stresses, the spatial, temporal, and quantitative variability observed in the distribution of discoid loomweights across and around the Aegean in the early centuries of the second millennium BCE most probably indicates several factors behind the spread of weaving fine, densely woven ground fabrics on warp-weighted looms that were invariably equipped with this type of loomweight (Cutler 2021, 247–249). The emulation of Cretan dress in the LC I insular communities has been considered as one of the primary causes of this phenomenon, while mobility of craftswomen through intermarriage is suggested as a likely mechanism of technological diffusion based on the premise that weaving was a highly gendered craft, performed by women (Gorogianni et al. 2015).

Although the occurrence of textile tools (spindle whorls) in male burials in the southern Greek Mainland (Nordquist 1987, 56) indicates that a gendered division of textile labour may not have been absolute across MBA Greece, one of the rare occasions where textile tools can possibly be associated with females is found at Ayia Irini on Kea. In a Middle Cycladic grave, an adolescent, most probably a girl, was buried with twenty-one spindle whorls (Overbeck 1989, 184, 198–199). Kea also provides support for the mobility of craftspeople. Macroscopic examination of the Ayia Irini discoid loomweights indicates that some tools were manufactured with non-local clays, and it is assumed that they had most probably been transported on Kea by their users when they relocated from other Aegean islands (Cutler 2021, 171–178). The same was observed at Akrotiri, Thera, where the textile tools recovered from MC deposits also include some specimens manufactured of non-local clays, both Cretan and non-Theran Cycladic (Vakirtzi 2019, macroscopic evaluations by J. Hilditch).

As mentioned before, emulation of Cretan dress fashion, at a time when the material culture of Crete influenced communities across the Aegean, has been suggested as the main motive for the adoption of Cretan weaving outside of Crete, given the representation of Cretan dress in the LC I frescoes of Thera (Cutler 2016a). However, accumulating evidence for the use of the Cretan warp-weighted loom early in the MC/MBA sequence, such as the early MC discoid loomweights found in Aegina and Thera, indicate that the adoption of Cretan ways of weaving predate the peak of the 'Minoanization' phenomenon by a few centuries. The lack of evidence on the type of garments used in the south Aegean islands during this period (see Section 2.2.1) does not encourage a correlation between weaving technological choices and clothing type. An alternative motive for the initial diffusion of the Cretan weaving technology in the Protopalatial period may have been the production of sailcloth (Vakirtzi 2019). This suggestion was based on the rough synchronization of the earliest iconographic evidence of the sailing ship in the Aegean (Figure 23) with the earliest occurrence of Cretan-type loomweights in harbour towns outside of Crete. Sailing ships are depicted on Cretan seals dated to the turn of the second millennium BCE (Broodbank 2013, 539), just about when Cretan-type, discoid loomweights turn up at Akrotiri on Thera and Kolonna on Aegina. If the sailing ship technology was first used by Cretans, then sails would have first been produced on Crete as well, perhaps on the warp-weighted loom equipped with discoid loomweights. Although this type of tool is suitable for the weaving of very dense, fine, and patterned cloth, it is also optimal for generic, 'ground weaves' (Cutler 2016a) and for 'cloths of greater width' (Burke 2010, 58). The hypothesis posits that soon after their adoption on

Clothing Bodies 45

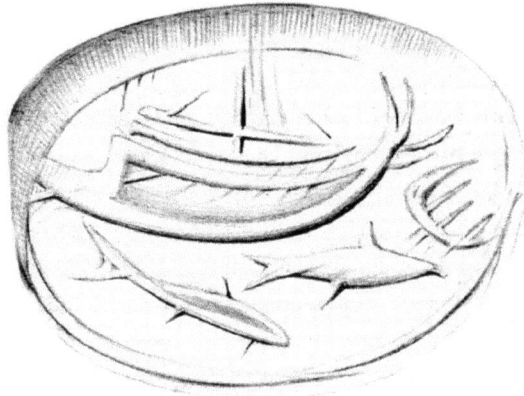

Figure 23 Sailing ship and fish, ivory seal from Platanos, Crete (CMS II.1.287b, image courtesy of the CMS Heidelberg).

Crete, sailing ships began to be built in other islands of the Aegean archipelago, and the weaving of sails followed the Cretan way of making textiles (Vakirtzi 2019).

This scenario does not rule out the use of discoid loomweights for other types of textiles, including those for garments. However, it inevitably links discoid loomweights with sailcloth and entails the question of whether weaving at Protopalatial Knossos was also targeting the production of sails. While the answer requires further research, what is certain is that textile production at Neopalatial Knossos shifted to a completely different focus, as evidenced by the shift to spherical loomweights, which are better suited to produce open or weft-faced fabrics (see Section 3.3.1). Nonetheless, Neopalatial coastal settlements such as Mochlos, Pseira, and Kommos produced textiles with discoid loomweights (Cutler et al. 2024, 731). These significant patterns that derive from the archaeological record of Neopalatial Crete will be discussed further in Section 3.3.1.

3.2.3 The Mainland

Textile Tools and Production Facilities

The influence of the MM weaving technology on Mainland Greece reached as far as Lerna, where a MH (Lerna phase V) settlement occupied the coast of the Argolic Gulf, in northeastern Peloponnese, following its EH III (Lerna phase IV) predecessor (Pullen 2008, 39). The site yielded three Cretan-type discoid loomweights from MH deposits (Banks 1967, 565–570). To date, no study of their ceramic fabric has been undertaken to evaluate whether these were locally made or transported to Lerna from another location.

There are no further reports of this loomweight type from the MH horizon. Moreover, a general scarcity of loomweights across the southern Mainland has been observed, with few exceptions. These include Asea in Arcadia, Eutresis in Boeotia, and Lianokladhi further north (Carington Smith 1975, 400–404). Asea and Eutresis yielded a few cylindrical loomweights and Lianokladhi spherical ones. No metric data are published, but the types imply rather thick tools that would be used to weave open or weft-faced cloth. In the south, at MH Malthi in Messenia the lack of identifiable loomweights contrasts sharply to the three hundred spindle whorls found across the site (Carington Smith 1975, 402–403; 1992, 689). It is assumed that the warp-weighted loom was not the dominant weaving technology in this settlement and instead a different type, perhaps the horizontal loom, would have been used. This is supported by the frequent occurrence at MH Peloponnesian sites of pierced clay spools with flaring shafts, like those discussed previously in the case of the MC settlements of Ayia Irini and Phylakopi, presumably used for reeling the warp before its arrangement on the horizontal loom (ibid., 404–410). They turn up in a variety of subtypes at several locations on the Peloponnese, in west Greece, and the southern Greek Mainland including Thessaly and Boeotia (Pavúk 2012).

In contrast to weaving, yarn manufacture is clearly documented owing to the assemblages of spindle whorls recovered at many MH sites, both in domestic and in funerary contexts (Carington Smith 1975, 356–400). Among the most securely dated assemblages are those originating from the two Peloponnesian sites of Malthi and Asine mentioned earlier, as well as from Eutresis in Boeotia. However, detailed reports of their typology and metric data are not available. For the spindle whorls of Asine, a weight range between 10 gr and 90 gr is mentioned (Nordquist 1987, 59), indicating a varied production of fine to coarse threads.

In the MH period the hollow-type spindle whorl decorated in an 'Anatolianizing' style, a standard tool in the whorl assemblages of the Eastern Aegean islands and the Cyclades from EC II to EC III onwards as discussed earlier, turns up on mainland sites. Carington Smith considered this as the 'hallmark' whorl type of the MH period (Carington Smith 1975, 352–353) and as diagnostic for the gradual mobility of population across a vast area encompassing central Asia through the Aegean (Carington Smith 1975, 356–389, 414–417). Barber further highlighted the westward appearance of this type of spindle whorl as far as north Italy and Switzerland, agreeing that these tools indicate patterns of familial mobility, based on the assumption that textile craft at that time was performed by women and girls (Barber 1991, 299–310). However, it is possible that making thread was not an exclusively female task in the Bronze Age Aegean, since spindle whorls occur in both male and female MH graves, for example at Asine in the Peloponnese (Nordquist 1987, 56).

Fragments of possible spinning bowls found in MH deposits at Nichoria, Messenia, in the southwestern Peloponnese were identified by Carington Smith (1992, 687). These implements have been interpreted as accessories for plying to make stronger spun or spliced threads. Their occurrence on the southern Mainland potentially indicates Cretan influence in thread-making technology, since spinning bowls were known in Crete as early as the EM period (Burke 2010, 28–29). In a recent article, Zavadil surveys more examples from Western Peloponnesian sites (Zavadil 2023). As mentioned in Section 3.1.3, she has questioned the use of this type of bowl for thread manufacture, primarily owing to the lack of diagnostic use wear traces in the Peloponnesian fragments. The same study, however, integrates the description of experiments that confirmed that this type of bowl can be effectively used to ply spliced linen threads (Zavadil 2023).

Excavated Textiles

Cloth remains preserved from MH Greece are extremely rare to date. A few, small, carbonized fragments were found in Kadmeia (Thebes, Boeotia) during a rescue excavation that is still unpublished (Margariti and Spantidaki 2023b, 21). However, the finds were submitted to radiocarbon dating with the results pointing to the early centuries of the second millennium BCE (Margariti and Spantidaki 2023b, 14–15), conventionally ascribed to the MH horizon. Even though their context remains obscure, the technical assessment of the fragments provides insights on textile craft. The weave is described as plain, rather balanced (Table 2). Bast fibre, possibly flax, was identified as the raw material. Margariti and Spantidaki make a case for the manufacture of the S-plied threads with the method of splicing instead of spinning, since the primary, single threads show 'very little twist' of a z direction, and the degree of twist in the plied thread is variable (Margariti and Spantidaki 2023b, 25).

The end of the MH period is marked by the earliest burials of Grave Circle B in Mycenae, with the latest tombs dated to LH I (Graziadio 1988). Given this Grave Circle's complex taphonomy, the textile fragments recovered from some of its tombs cannot be readily attributed to the earlier or the later phases of its use, and will therefore be discussed in the next section devoted to the early Late Bronze Age.

3.3 The Late Bronze Age–Early

3.3.1 Neopalatial Crete

Excavated Textiles

In contrast to the wealth of representations of clothing, excavated textiles from Neopalatial Crete remain very few. The most thoroughly studied case of Neopalatial Crete consists of *c.* 20 fragments belonging to the same textile, a narrow weft-faced cloth band (Table 2) preserved in carbonized state (Möller-Wiering 2006). The find originates from the multi-period site at Kastelli, Chania, West Crete (Bruun-Lundgren et al. 2015). It was recovered from House IV, a building destroyed by conflagration in the LM IB period. The cloth fragments were resting inside a tripod pyxis found on the floor of Room C of the house (Evely 2010, 195). The estimated size of the surviving band, when all fragments are taken into consideration, is 6 mm wide to 9 cm long, making this textile the earliest example of a narrow cloth band found in the Aegean so far. S. Möller-Wiering (2006), who performed a technological analysis of the find, has highlighted a number of technical features that suggest, in her opinion, that the manufacturing technique of this band was plaiting rather than weaving. The threads of both systems, where visible, barely show any spin, at best a loose primary twist. The wefts appear to have been inserted as bundles, rather than continuously. This textile manifests the combination of three different fibres: the warp, which is double S-plied, is linen, the weft, showing minimal twist, was made of goat hair, while a supplementary, double S-plied thread made of nettle was used as a decorative or strengthening element (stitch) in the basic plaited structure (Moulhérat and Spantidaki 2009).

A second Neopalatial textile artefact found at Zakros, East Crete, was published in a preliminary report (Platon 1972, 178). It consists of the mineralized remains of a textile plaited in a 'herringbone' structure. It was traced during the excavation of the Neopalatial 'Building North of the Harbour Street'. The excavator identified the textile as 'cloth or mat' (Platon 1972, 178). A decisive criterion for its technological classification would be the morphology of the warps and wefts: if they are plant strips, the find qualifies as a product of matting. If they are threads, either spun or spliced, this would justify its classification as cloth.[4]

The two (probably plaited) artefacts from Neopalatial Crete just discussed, testify to textile manufacturing techniques and fibre-made artefacts complementary to those woven on the warp-weighted looms that were used all over Crete. Although the demonstration of local (Chaniote, or even Cretan)

---

[4] The Zakros plaited artefact has been studied by E. Gerontakou, who is currently preparing its publication.

production is not self-evident, the narrow textile band of Kastelli brings the textile evidence closer to the iconographic evidence. In the repertoire of garment representation, the bodices, skirts, and kilts with elaborate ornamentations are often decorated with narrow, patterned bands on the sleeves, or the hems of kilts and skirts (Barber 1991, 314–322) (Figures 7 and 8). The find from Kastelli, Chania, is the first tangible testimony of the craftsmanship invested in creating such textile bands.

Textile Tools and Production Facilities

Textile production in Neopalatial Crete is attested through loomweights, spindle whorls, and other production implements (needles, spinning bowls) found at various types of sites across the island: in buildings near palatial centres, in the building complexes defined as 'villas', in town houses, and in smaller, 'rural' settlements. In some cases, evidence of weaving occurs in special, non-domestic contexts, such as Building 4 at the funerary complex at Phourni, and 'the sanctuary' of Anemospilia, both in Archanes (Sakellarakis and Sapouna-Sakellaraki 1997, 319–320). Facilities identified as basins to wash the fibres or for dye production are also attested (Alberti 2007). The relevant evidence has been synthesized in several studies resulting in a voluminous body of work (most notably, Burke 2010; Militello 2014a; Cutler 2021). As a general remark, it could be noted that cloth production occupied an important place in people's lives and that textile industries were a crucial facet of Neopalatial household and political economies (Burke 2010, Militello 2014a, 264–265).

Regarding thread manufacture, the pattern of spindle whorl scarcity, observed in the Protopalatial period, persists. Spindle whorls have occasionally been reported, however, giving the impression of small-scale thread manufacture. Most scholars think that thread would have likely been manufactured with more than the spinning technique, or that whorls would have been made of wood therefore have not survived (Burke 2010; Cutler 2021). It is quite likely that plying thread was practiced in some locations with the use of spinning bowls, for example, at Ayia Triada (Militello 2014a, 135–138), continuing a Prepalatial and Protopalatial technical tradition (Burke 2010, 29). Some of the few Neopalatial locations that yielded low numbers of whorls include Ayios Syllas and Sklavokampos in north-central Crete; the building at Chalara and the 'villa' of Ayia Triada, both near Phaistos; Sissi, where one steatite spindle whorl was found; and Kastelli in Chania, where, again, just one spindle whorl is reported from House I (Cutler 2021, 108, 112–113, 138, 157–158). When weight values are reported, they correspond to light spindle whorls, indicating production orientated to rather fine threads (Cutler 2021). The group of ten spindle whorls found at Archanes appears to be an exceptional case of a small assemblage of thread-making tools manufactured of precious stones (Sakellarakis and Sapouna-Sakellaraki 1997, 85).

A change can be observed in the organization of 'palatial' production, as weaving workshops are no longer located within palatial complexes, but rather in nearby buildings in the vicinity of palaces. This is the case both at Knossos (Cutler 2021) and Phaistos (Militello 2014a). But perhaps the most notable shift regards the type of textiles that were being produced, notably in Neopalatial Knossos, where the focus was on the production of open, probably weft-faced textiles, as indicated by the dominance of the spherical type of loomweight (Figure 11, d) in assemblages recovered from locations around the palatial complex (Cutler 2021, 74–100). It should be reminded that weaving with this type of loomweights was very common at Protopalatial Malia, at a time when only discoid loomweights were used at Knossos, probably for weaving dense, fine fabrics. In the Neopalatial period, however, this type of textiles is no longer produced in Knossos, but apparently in 'villas' such as Sklavokampos, towns such as Tylissos (where also spherical loomweights are documented), as well as coastal settlements like Kommos, Mochlos, and Pseira, where discoid loomweights were found (Cutler 2021, 108, 113–117, 139–141).

Spherical loomweights also dominate the weaving toolkit found at the building complex of Tourkogeitonia in Archanes and at the 'villa' of Vathypetro. At Kastelli, Chania, in west Crete, the Neopalatial House I accommodated a weaving workshop, judging from the many loomweights found therein, most of which were spherical (Cutler 2021, 106–108, 157). It is interesting that some of these were found on the floors of Rooms M and E. In one case, the spatial distribution of the tools and the recovery of organic material identified as burnt wood from the same area, suggest the identification of a loom that was set-up when the house was abandoned (Bruun-Luundgren et al. 2015, 199–200, Fig. 6.2.4). At Phaistos, textile production in the palatial complex ceased and a textile industry was instead established at the 'villa' of Ayia Triada in the Neopalatial phase. Weaving here relied on spherical loomweights; therefore, the main target of textile production would have been open or weft-faced types of cloth. There are no examples of the cylindrical loomweight type that was common in Protopalatial Phaistos, so that a shift in textile production can be surmised in this case, too. Moreover, the recovery of a few discoid loomweights indicate that fine, densely woven cloth could also have been produced (Militello 2014a, 255–256; Cutler 2021, 112–113).

The reorientation of the textile production in (or around) the major palatial centres towards targets different from those of the previous period, as well as the broader picture of a widely diversified production on an insular scale, considering the overall variety of loomweight types found throughout the island, constitute the two main characteristics of Neopalatial Cretan weaving. This picture contrasts sharply to the one emerging from the rest of the insular Aegean, as will be discussed in the next section.

3.3.2 The Insular Region

Textile Tools and Production Facilities

One of the earliest excavations of an insular LC I settlement to yield textile implements was that of Phylakopi in Melos in the late 19th century CE, even though at the time there was some ambiguity as to their exact use (Cutler et al. 2024). Those early finds of Phylakopi were consequently identified as loomweights of the Cretan, discoid type, but their attribution in the site's stratigraphy is problematic (Cutler et al. 2024). From the well-stratified deposits that were investigated with trial trenches in the 1970s campaign (Renfrew et al. 2007), only two fragmentary Cretan-type, discoid loomweights were recovered from Phase D deposits corresponding to the LC I/II. Thus, weaving on the warp-weighted loom is not well documented, although thread production was certainly taking place in Phylakopi in this period, as indicated by spindle whorls (Cherry and Davis 2007, 401–410).

Following the launch of excavations at two other emblematic Cycladic settlements, Ayia Irini on Kea and Akrotiri on Thera, batches of Cretan-type, discoid loomweights began to come up from LC I deposits, manifesting the continued use of the Cretan weaving technology in the insular region. Weaving industries are well attested at both sites, specifically in the large building defined as House A at Ayia Irini (Cummer and Schofield 1984; Cutler 2021, 182–216) and in the West House of Akrotiri on Thera (Tzachili 1997; 2007a), both of which probably accommodated many looms, given the large amounts of tools found therein. Archaeological research elsewhere in the Aegean yielded similar finds at sites expanding from Kythera to Rhodes, and from Karpathos to Samothrace (Cutler 2021; Nikolakopoulou 2022, 143).

The more it became clear that Cretan-type, discoid loomweights are the dominant loom implement in the weaving landscape of the insular Aegean, the more weaving practices became part of the discussion on 'Minoanization' (e.g., Davis 1984), eventually receiving the attention of a specialist treatment by J. Cutler (2021) who suggested that these loomweights in some cases represent the first adoption of the warp-weighted loom technology outside of Crete. Following a thorough analysis of the textile-related archaeological record of the second-millennium-BCE Aegean, Cutler's study demonstrates variations in the timing and scale of the appearance of Cretan, discoid loomweights in insular settlements. Moreover, Cutler highlighted the multi-directional trajectories that the Cretan influence took, based on a 'wide variety of non-local fabrics' used for the manufacture of textile tools (Cutler 2021, 258). Although her analysis suggests that the phenomenon of 'Minoanization', weaving included, should be 'unpacked' into multiple processes, agents, and driving forces, the study underlines female mobility as a core mechanism of textile technology diffusion (Gorogianni et al. 2015; Cutler 2021, 257–258). In this respect, Cutler followed a basic premise in the studies of E. Barber (1991) and I. Tzachili (1997), both of whom underlined the gendered division of textile labour cross-culturally and diachronically, to argue that thread manufacture and weaving in the Bronze Age Aegean, too, had been primarily 'women's work'.

Tzachili's research, focusing on Akrotiri, Thera, was undertaken as a case study of how textile production was organized in an Aegean harbour town of the LC I period (Tzachili 1997; 2007a; 2007b). The exceptionally well-preserved Theran town offers the potential for informing our interpretations of the material record with details not widely available elsewhere in the Aegean. Textile tools and especially loomweights of the Cretan, discoid type attest to the use of the warp-weighted loom. However, in the LC phase of Akrotiri this technology should be considered local rather than a foreign influence, since it had been in use for several generations from the beginning of the second millennium (MC Phase A) onwards (Vakirtzi 2019).

By analysing the textile tools and their distribution, Tzachili demonstrated the technical and social characteristics of the craft, that is, that cloth production was highly standardized and carried out only in some of the town's houses (Tzachili 1997, 2007b). In just one building, the West House, about four hundred discoid loomweights were kept, indicating a scale of production that exceeded the household's needs (Tzachili 2007a). A detailed stratigraphic and taphonomic analysis showed that weaving workshops were located in large, well-lit rooms, on the houses' upper floors (Tzachili 1997) (Supplementary Figure 7). The recovery of Linear A documents listing about two hundred textiles from one of the town's building complexes, Complex Delta, suggests that the textile industry of Akrotiri would have been orientated towards some sort of exchange or trade transactions (Boulotis 2008). The targets of this production would have been densely woven fabrics of rather balanced weaves (Tzachili et al. 2015), based on the functional analysis of discoid loomweights. However, following the early 2000s excavation project at Akrotiri, the 'Pillar Pits' excavation (Doumas 2021) there is evidence that textile production would not have been so strictly standardized as once thought. From the 'Pillar Pits' excavations, a few Cretan-type loomweights of the spherical variety were recovered from LC I deposits (Tzachili 2021). These demonstrate that, even if at a smaller scale, Akrotiri weavers were also engaged in cloth production similar to that of Neopalatial Knossos, Archanes, Kastelli-Chania, and the other weaving centres of Crete where spherical loomweights were traced. This type of production would have targeted the type of open weave, weft-faced textiles which were largely confined to Crete.

The 'Pillar Pit' excavations also yielded spindle whorls. Thread production at Akrotiri had previously been considered dubious (Tzachili 1990), given the scarcity of these tools in the West House (Tzachli 2007a). These are less than ten, while the house accommodated c. 400 loomweights. They are thus too few to produce the amounts of yarn needed for the many looms of the house. It was therefore suggested that yarn would have been locally produced with tools not identifiable archaeologically, and/or that it would have been imported from elsewhere (Tzachili 1990). When all the whorls recovered from LC deposits, including recent finds from the 'Pillar Pits', are considered (Vakirtzi 2015; Vakirtzi 2021) the pattern of small-scale thread-making is reinforced. In many instances they were found in secondary deposits (backfilling, building material, destruction debris) which is not surprising given the more than one destruction that the LC town underwent and the ensuing rebuilding activities, before the volcanic eruption (Nikolakopoulou 2003). It appears that spinning within the town would have been a routine task aiming to provide at least some of the yarn used for weaving. The spindle whorls recovered from the town are manufactured of clay and stone in a range of types and sizes from very small to large: the weight values of complete or almost complete tools range from almost 3 to 33 gr (Vakirtzi 2012; Vakirtzi 2015). This range indicates a varied thread production, including very fine threads. These could have been woollen or linen. Indeed, both textile materials are directly attested at Akrotiri demonstrating that the town was consuming such textiles and the inhabitants were familiar with fine linen and woollen cloth (see further, *Excavated Textiles*). Other materials might also have been used. Perhaps one of these was wild silk, as suggested by the recovery of a calcified moth cocoon from the town, attributed to a butterfly species that is known as a source of this type of fibre (Panagiotakopulu et al. 1997). Ethnographic studies indicate that the manufacture of thread from wild silk requires spinning, unlike cultivated silk, in order to create a long filament from the short, cut fibres that remain on the broken cocoon after the insect has escaped it (Douny 2013). Some of the lightest and smallest spindle whorls of Akrotiri may well have been used to this purpose (Vakirtzi 2012).

Excavated Textiles

A small corpus of textile fragments originates from the 'Pillar Pits' excavation. By Aegean standards, textiles at Akrotiri were preserved in relatively good condition, along with several other artefacts made of organic materials (Michaelidis and Angelidis 2006). The published corpus consists of three different textiles found in Pillar Pit 68A, Pillar Pit 1B, and Pillar Pit 52N (Figure 24a-c, Table 2). The textile fragments were studied by Youlie Spantidaki and Christophe Moulhérat (2021) who conducted technical analyses of the threads and weaves, as well as fibre identification.

The textile from Pillar Pit 68A is a carbonized fragment in a plain, open, weft-faced weave. At least three different types of threads were used for its manufacture, an S-plied linen warp, a single z-twisted weft, and thicker threads used presumably as side seams (Spantidaki and Moulhérat 2021, 242–245). The weft remains to be determined as to the exact plant species.

The textile fragment of Pillar Pit 1B was found carbonized in a mass of burnt barley grain and was interpreted as a sack (Spantidaki and Moulhérat 2021). It is woven in a plain weave, with double 2-plied warp threads of plant origin and unspun/flat wefts, suggested to be vegetal strips (Spantidaki and Moulhérat

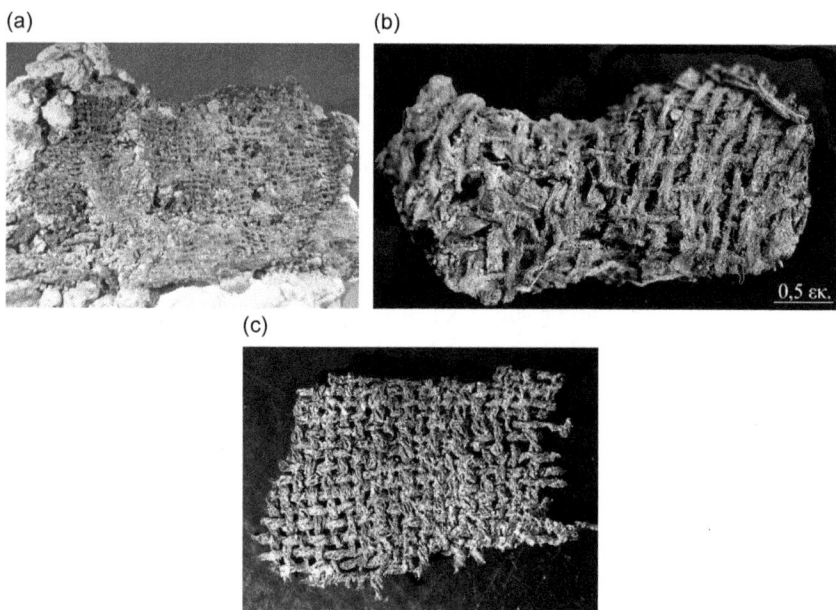

Figure 24a Textile from Pillar Pit 68A, Akrotiri, Thera.
b Textile fragment from Pillar Pit 1B, Akrotiri, Thera.
c Textile fragment from Pillar Pit 52N, Akrotiri, Thera (images courtesy of Akrotiri Excavations ©Akrotiri Excavations/Society for the Promotion of Theran Studies).

2021, 246–247). No further identification of the exact plant species for the warp or the weft was possible. Technologically, it manifests a combination of woven cloth and plaited mat, and as Spantidaki and Moulhérat have pointed out, it presents us with the challenge to recognize the technique or the device with which it would have been created.

The finest textile published from Akrotiri to date was recovered from Pillar Pit 52 N in several small carbonized pieces, some of which were found folded. Careful observation of their technical characteristics indicated that all fragments belonged to the same cloth. The raw material was determined to be flax. The threads in both systems are double S-plied while the weave structure is plain and balanced (Spantidaki and Moulhérat 2021, 237). Supplementary threads on the ground weave were diagnosed as embroidery, tassels, or a possible seam, sewn with a thread that is thicker than those of the ground fabric (Spantidaki and Moulhérat 2021, 239–242). Knots of various sizes were created to stabilize the edge of the warp system, a technical feature common in Egyptian textiles of the New Kingdom (Kemp and Vogelsang-Eastwood 2001, 133–144, Fig. 4.55).

Of the three, different findspots of the excavated textiles, the area of Pillar Pit 68A has not yet been published; therefore, the context of the textile remains to be determined. However, the space revealed in 1B was studied by a team of scholars who recognized a cooking area there (Birtacha 2008, 390–391). The textile fragments of Pillar Pit 52 N were scattered in a pile of hundreds of horns, mostly of sheep and goats, next to a clay box enclosing a golden, ibex figurine (Alexopoulos 2021). Subsequent research in this area has shown that this space was the interior of a room, while the excavation of a second room next to it revealed textile and thread imprints in proximity to an assemblage of metal and ceramic artefacts and beads, including one with a fragment of red thread in its hole (Doumas 2019, 288; Birtacha forthcoming).

The technical features of the cloth fragments found at Akrotiri raise the question of their compatibility with the textile technology used at the site in the LC I period. As discussed earlier, the spindle whorls found scattered in the town manifest a range of sizes. Spindle whorls as light as 4–8 gr were used in experimental spinning at CTR and were proven functional, producing thread qualities comparable to those of the Akrotiri textiles (Möller-Wiering 2015). These spindle whorls could also have been used to manufacture wool threads, like those found in a carbonized state at Akrotiri (Moulhérat and Spantidaki 2008). Such fine threads could have been woven in plain, balanced types of fabrics, in any of the four textile workshops identified so far in the Late Cycladic town, equipped with discoid loomweights (Tzachili 2007b). Thicker threads could have been used as wefts, for embroidery or in weaving with heavier, spherical loomweights. Plied yarns could have been made with spindles equipped with whorls such as those locally found. It could therefore be suggested that the textile tools and the cloth fragments found at Akrotiri are generally compatible. Yet, a growing corpus of technical studies of extant textiles from the Eastern Mediterranean, including Egyptian ones (Andersson Strand and Nosch 2015, Appendix B), demonstrates that the craftsmanship manifest in the cloth fragments of Akrotiri was a widespread achievement in the wider region during the second millennium BCE. Based on the aforementioned remarks, while the local production of the textiles found at Akrotiri appears entirely feasible from a technological perspective, it cannot be ruled out that any of these items may have arrived in Thera from another region of the Aegean or even the Eastern Mediterranean.

3.3.3 The Mainland, LH I–II

Excavated Textiles

The LC I textiles of Akrotiri find contemporary parallels on Mainland Greece, excavated in funerary contexts. An assemblage of textiles is known from Grave Circles A and B of Mycenae. In Grave Circle B, several cloth fragments were preserved in Tombs A, B, Γ, Δ, and N (Mylonas 1972–1973, 22, 38, 49, 81, 88, 162, 171–172): some of these textiles were used to 'clothe' or contain weapons such as metal swords (Tomb Γ), arrowheads (Tomb Δ), a spearhead, a dagger, and a knife (Tomb N), while others were found on metal vessels (Tomb A) or around ceramic ones (Tomb B). The published photographs of the cloth fragments found in Tombs A and B suggest plain, balanced ground weaves (Mylonas 1972–1973, Plates 20b, 25) (Figure 25a-b). The textiles that wrapped the spearhead, the dagger and the knife of Tomb N were studied by Y. Spantidaki and C. Moulhérat and were determined to be linen, woven with double threads with S-twist direction, in a plain, balanced weave with a count of 20–22 threads per sq. cm (Spantidaki and Moulhérat 2012, 192) (Table 2). From Grave Circle A, a few fragments of textiles have been published, found in Graves II and V (Karo 1930–1933, 71, 137, 142, 145, Taf. CXLVI).

The textile corpus of the Grave Circles is currently under study, integrating both a technical analysis of the textiles and an archaeometric determination of the raw materials, from fibres to dyes. Preliminary results suggest a variety of weaving techniques employed for their manufacture, ranging from the ubiquitous plain weave, to weft-faced textiles including tapestry, while purple dye has been traced on some of these textiles (Spantidaki 2022).

Tapestry weaving is rarely encountered even in what constitutes the largest corpus of Bronze Age textiles from the Eastern Mediterranean, that

Clothing Bodies 57

Figure 25a Textile fragments from Grave A, Grave Circle B, Mycenae, Argolid
b Textile fragments from Grave B, Grave Circle B, Mycenae, Argolid
(images reproduced from Mylonas 1973, Vol. B, Pl. 20b, 25 ©The Athens Archaeological Society).

is, that of New Kingdom Egypt (Kemp and Vogelsang-Eastwood 2001, 89; Spinazzi-Lucchesi 2018, 80). In the Egyptian context, too, cloth woven in the tapestry technique originates from royal or elite tombs of the 18th Dynasty and are considered Syrian-inspired, while a few have been determined as imports (Smith 2013, 163, 176). Their appearance in the material record of the 18th Dynasty has been associated with the military campaign of the Pharaoh Thutmose III against Megiddo and the captivity of Syrian artisans (Barber 1991, 157–158). The Mycenaean find should be considered as the earliest Bronze Age tapestry in the Eastern Mediterranean to have been found, so far, outside of Egypt (Appendix B, Andersson Strand and Nosch 2015). Its occurrence in the Grave Circles raises the question of textile craft influences between Mycenae and other locations in the Eastern Mediterranean during the Shaft Grave period (Cline 1994, 9–24, 106), given the Syrian and Egyptian connotations of the Bronze Age tapestry technique and the long-distance exchange networks that emerged during this period (Murray 2023, 29).

In the Argolid a few more textile fragments were traced in the richly furnished LH II Tholos Tomb of Kazarma (de Wild 2001, 115) while a bowl that was among the contents of chamber tomb 2 at the Mycenaean cemetery of Dendra, retained 'a large piece of Mycenaean cloth' (Persson 1931, 77) described as plain weave by de Wild (2001, 115).

In Messenia, southwestern Peloponnese, textile remains were preserved among the grave goods of the lavishly furnished burial of the so-called 'Griffin Warrior' (Davis and Stocker 2016, 632), closely dated to the LH IIA period (Stocker et al. 2022). This material, currently under study for publication, will add important insight to our understanding of funerary textiles use associated with an undisturbed, male burial.

Some more evidence from this period originates from Boeotia. Fragments of a funerary textile were preserved in one of the tombs excavated within the so-called 'Blue Stone Structure' complex, dated to the transitional MH III-LH I period at Eleon (Burke and Dimova 2023). Preliminary analysis attributed all of the fragments to the same cloth, based on a consistent warp count. The weave is described as weft-faced, because the weft count is always greater than the warp count (Table 2). Holes of up to 1.6 mm in diameter, in a diagonal arrangement, are considered as indications of supplementary weft. The analysis of the fibres under the SEM was inconclusive as to their identification, due to the degradation of the material. However, according to the study team the raw material was probably wool, based on the thread structure (single, z-twist) and the fibre diameters (Burke and Dimova 2023, 15).

Textile Tools and Production Facilities

Identification of evidence for textile production during the early LB period in southern Mainland Greece is challenging, owing to the scarcity of well-preserved and adequately excavated settlements: the period is much more documented through surface surveys and excavations of burial sites, while at multi-period sites, the LH I–II horizons are, as a rule, only partially preserved due to the building that took place in the mature Mycenaean phase (Wright 2008). Since the material culture of this period is much more documented through burial contexts (Crowley 2008), there is a bias in favour of the representation of the tools of thread manufacture, because spindle whorls were often deposited in or around tombs (e.g., Tomb O, in Circle Grave B, Mylonas 1972–1973, 353, Pl. 189) (Supplementary Figure 8) as opposed to loomweights. To date, the most comprehensive, synthetic work on LBA textile tools from the Greek Mainland remains that of Carington Smith (1975), but her study treats the LBA as a whole and does not distinguish between the earlier and later periods. Even so, however, the scarcity of loomweights, especially in the southern region, is noted (Carington Smith 1975, 446–457), usually interpreted as negative evidence for the preferred use of loom types other than the warp-weighted loom. Exceptions that change this impression are noted in the settlement of Nichoria in Messenia. Twelve clay loomweights, including two of the discoid, Cretan-type, the rest of a variety of other shapes, were found there in mixed LH II/III deposits (Carington Smith 1992, 687). Nine of these were found in a dump deposit that Carington Smith attributed to an 'early Mycenaean' building that would have contained one loom (Carington Smith 1992, 688). The *c.* 180 spindle whorls recovered from Nichoria are also attributed to mixed MBA/LBA deposits. Nonetheless they are an indication of the continued importance of yarn industries in the region, earlier documented at MH Malthi (see Section 3.2.3).

The earliest examples of steatite 'conuli', or 'buttons', a hallmark of Mycenaean material culture, are dated in this period, as is indicated by examples found also at Nichoria (Carington Smith 1992, 685–686). This artefact class includes small, centrally pierced cones with straight sides (and a few variations of this shape) that resemble conical whorls. Although some scholars have refuted their use for spinning on the grounds of their size, the diameter of the central hole, or their contextual associations in burials (Carington Smith 1992; Iakovidis 1977), a recent examination of a sample of those indicates that some were manufactured in shapes and sizes compatible with the whorl use, while surface wear typical of spindle whorls has been observed as well (Vakirtzi 2015). Thus, in some cases the spindle whorl identification is possible. These artefacts are often found along with clay spindle whorls and loomweights in deposits dating from the mature Mycenaean phase, reinforcing such an interpretation.

3.4 The Late Bronze Age–Late

3.4.1 Crete, Final Palatial, and Postpalatial Periods

Excavated Textiles and Imprints

The few cloth fragments that can be dated within this timespan preserve nothing that echoes the sophisticated, specialized textile industry conveyed by the Mycenaean documents found on Crete, specifically in Knossos (Nosch 2024). Extant textiles include: the clay imprint of a textile from 'post-LM II contexts' found in the Unexplored Mansion, Knossos (Popham et al. 1984, pl. 222.5) which manifests plain weave according to de Wild (2001, 115); small pieces of a mineralized cloth adhering on one of the swords found in the 'Chieftain's Grave' at the cemetery of Zafer Papoura, Knossos, which Evans described as linen (Evans 1935, 866–867), and E. Barber suggested is an open, plain weave (Barber 1991, 174, n. 12); and another mineralized fragment preserved on a metal vessel found in a LM IIIB tomb at Chania, showing plain weave (Karantzali 1986, p. 75, Fig. 17).

Textile Tools and Production Facilities

Knossos was the administrative centre of a large-scale, well-organized textile industry during the Final Palatial period, relying primarily on wool, but also targeting linen textiles. This industry was closely controlled and recorded on clay tablets in the Linear B script, thus testifying to the administrative practices of Greek-speaking (and writing) scribes on Crete (Killen 2007). The documents of Knossos convey the full cycle of the production, from managing herds of sheep destined for wool husbandry (Killen 2007), to distributing the raw wool to workers located at places other than Knossos, to spinning, weaving, returning several different types of finished cloth, and possibly storing them, at least for some time, at Knossos (Del Freo et al. 2010). The territory involved in wool husbandry, and the craft centres where this decentralized manufacture was taking place, have been identified in some cases, based on analyses of place-names and the 'ethnic' adjectives of textile workers, mentioned in the tablets (Killen 2007; Bennet 2024). The Knossian textile industry was extremely specialized, as indicated by the many terms used in the texts to describe several different 'professions' within the production cycle. Moreover, for the first time in the Aegean Bronze Age, textile craft appears as a clearly gendered sector, a women's sphere of work (Killen 2007; Del Freo et al. 2010), at least in the palatial industries.

The study of textile implements contributes to the identification of several facets of Cretan textile production in the Final and Postpalatial periods. In the area of Knossos textile tools from LM II/IIIA-B deposits were found in spaces outside the main palatial complex, but also *again in* the palace, after a Neopalatial break (Cutler 2021, 72). LM II–III deposits with mixed loom-weight types, but with the spherical type dominating, were found in the Royal Road South and the Royal Road North, the South House, at Gypsadhes, at the Unexplored Mansion, and the Southwest Houses (Cutler 2021, 74–75, 85, 91–92, 98). The frequency and the dominance of the spherical loomweight type suggest a level of continuity from the previous period, despite the destructions at the end of the Neopalatial era. A notable difference from the Neopalatial record is the co-occurrence of spindle whorls in some of the same areas, especially in contexts dated to LM III (Cutler 2021). In LM III deposits there is a new element in the typological repertoire of tools found in the palace and the Unexplored Mansion, namely unpierced clay spools (Figure 26). This type should not be confused with the perforated spool type with flaring shafts known from the Middle Bronze Age horizon. The identification of these unpierced spools as loomweights was suggested by Barber (1997, see further)

Figure 26 Drawings of some unpierced clay spools from Ayia Triada (image courtesy of P. Militello 2014a, Pl. XXIII ©P. Militello).

while their efficacy for weaving has been confirmed experimentally (Barber 1997; Andersson Strand and Nosch 2015; Siennicka and Ulanowska 2016).

Elsewhere on Crete, textile tools from contexts dated to the LM II and LM III periods are noted from Kommos, where the discoid loomweight type continued to be used almost exclusively (Cutler 2021, 113–117). At Palaikastro, deposits attributed to the LM II and LM III periods from Building I contained a mix of loomweight types (Cutler 2021, 155), known from earlier phases but now also including the unpierced spool type, while LM IIIC deposits excavated in trial trenches at Kastri, Palaikastro, also yielded clay spools (Cutler 2021, 151). Spools were also encountered in LM IIIB-C contexts at Kastelli, Chania, along with discoid, and possibly stone loomweights as well (Bruun-Lundgren et al. 2015, 199, 203). Over sixty spindle whorls found at Kastelli were attributed to LM IIIB-C deposits, most of which are small and light and therefore suitable for fine thread production (Bruun-Lundgren et al. 2015, 204). These finds add to the Knossian pattern that indicates both stages of the operational sequence of textile production, thread making and weaving, taking place in the same location within urban centres. At Ayia Triada in the Mesara, weaving is represented by a few discoid and spherical loomweights and unpierced clay spools (Militello 2014a, 257). Fine thread production is indicated during the LM IIIA/IIIB periods by small and light spindle whorls made in clay or stone in the 'conuli' shape. The latter is regarded by Militello as a more 'prestigious' type of whorl (Militello 2014a, 256). Prestige in spinning at Phaistos may also be inferred by the deposition of ivory spindles in LM IIIC burials at Kalyvia (Militello 2014a, 267), assuming that the consumption of ivory artefacts can be considered as an indication of luxury (but *cf.* Murray 2018 for a different opinion). The spindles of Kalyvia are just ivory rods, no whorls were preserved, unlike their contemporary counterparts recovered at the LH IIIC cemetery at Perati, Attica, on the Greek Mainland (see Section 3.4.2).

The continuity of the weaving choices of the Neopalatial period, exemplified by the undisrupted dominance of the spherical loomweight at Final Palatial Knossos, is noteworthy given the 'Mycenaean' administration that was established there and kept record of the textile industry. More generally, Final and Postpalatial textile production on Crete is noted for the increased representation of spindle whorls in the archaeological deposits, in sharp contrast to the Neopalatial pattern; and for the emergence of the unpierced clay spool as a new type of loomweight across Crete. Textile craft in the transition from the Neopalatial to the Final, and ultimately to the Postpalatial period, requires further research to explore these patterns, especially given the wealth of information afforded by the Mycenaean records found on Crete. Spools, however, have caught the attention of E. Barber, who suggested that their function as a special type of loomweight can be supported by ethnographic parallels and based on the results of experimental weaving (Barber 1997). She argued that this sort of weaving may have been particularly effective in producing patterned bands that could then be sewn into the multicoloured, Cretan kilts represented in the wall-paintings (Figure 8). She also associated the origin of this type of narrow band weaving to 'nomadic or semi-nomadic herders on the steppes – the area and lifestyle from which the Indo-European Hittites and Mycenaean Greeks arrived in the North Mediterranean in the second millennium BCE' (Barber 1997, 517). However, as their contexts suggest, unpierced clay spools mark the end of the Mycenaean palatial period rather than its beginning.

3.4.2 The Insular Region

Excavated Textiles and Imprints

Mycenaean-era excavated textiles from the insular region have been reported from the island of Rhodes and the cemetery of Aspropilia at Pylona (LH IIIA2-LH IIIB1), specifically from tombs 1 and 2 C (Karantzali 2001). Tomb 1 contained a rich burial that included the skeletal remains of one man and two women, furnished with jewellery, metal artefacts, and thirty clay vessels. Among those, two large piriform jars and one jug preserved textile remains. One of the female skeletons also preserved linen textile fragments on the forehead, jaw and forearm, interpreted by the excavator as a 'funerary band ... fastened around the dead person's jaw and skull ... to secure the mouth' (Karantzali 2001, 15). The textiles of tomb 1 were preserved in a calcified state, in layers and folds. De Wild analysed the cloth remains and observed plain weave structures, with subtle differences in the thread counts (Table 2) (de Wild 2001, 114–115). The threads have an s -twist, but it is not clarified if they are single or plied. The fibre is suggested to be flax in all cases, although the method or criteria of identification are not elaborated. These textiles had been used to seal the mouths of the respective ceramic vessels (de Wild 2001, 114; Karantzali 2001, Cpl. 2, pl. 27b-e, pl. 34a-d, pl. 51), exemplifying a more 'mundane' or 'industrial' use of cloth in daily activities.

Textile Tools and Production Facilities

At Phylakopi, on the island of Melos, two buildings attributed to the Mycenaean period have been excavated, the Megaron (phases E-F, Renfrew 2007, 9–13) and the Mycenaean Sanctuary (Renfrew 1985), the latter better preserved and documented (Supplementary Figure 9). From the stratigraphical trenches of the 1970s, less than five fragmentary loomweights, all belonging to the Cretan discoid type were found, mainly in the Megaron area, in secondary deposits attributed to Phases E and F (Cherry and Davis 2007, 403–405). In the Mycenaean Sanctuary some more fragmentary loomweights of the Cretan discoid type were collected from deposits corresponding to the various phases identified in the building sequence (Renfrew 1985, 71–80, 331, 336). Spindle whorls have a limited representation in LH III deposits from the Megaron area (Cherry and Davis 2007, 408, Table 10.1) and most of those recovered from the Sanctuary were in destruction debris or building fills. Nonetheless, some were found in primary deposition on floors, on or near the platforms of the Shrine, as part of the 'Assemblages' of votive offerings located there (Assemblages A, B, K and L, Renfrew 1985, passim). Within these contexts there are clay spindle whorls, in good preservation and in various types and sizes (Figure 27a-c), including small ones weighing less than 10 gr (Vakirtzi 2015).

Ayia Irini on Kea is the second Cycladic settlement to provide evidence of textile craft during the Mycenaean phase (phase VIII). However, these deposits are neither extensive nor rich in textile tools. Only a few loomweights of the Cretan discoid type have been attributed to LH III (Cutler 2021, 188–189, 203) raising the question of the scale of production, in contrast to spindle whorls that are more numerous and more widely distributed in this horizon (Cutler 2021, 169–215, passim).

At Naxos, in the Cyclades, an urban centre was founded in Grotta in the Mycenaean period and flourished throughout the LC IIIC phase (Vlachopoulos 2019). The settlement, traced beneath the modern town of Naxos, was partially excavated, preserving part of the city wall as well as domestic areas adjacent to it. Among those was a small room filled with destruction debris where two ivory spindles were found, one of which retained its whorl (Lambrinoudakis and Zafeiropoulou 1984, 324). These finds demonstrate that textile equipment made

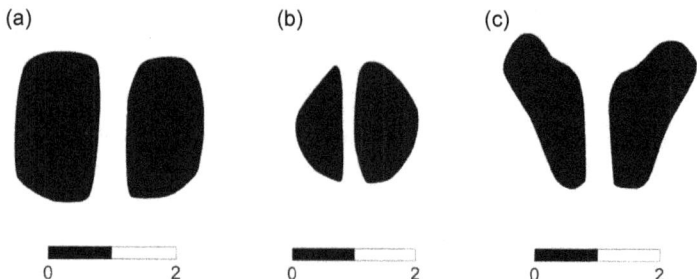

Figure 27a-c Types of spindle whorls found on or near the platforms of the West Shrine at the Mycenaean Sanctuary of Phylakopi, Melos: a. cylindrical b. spheroid c. conical with concave sides and hollow top (drawings by S. Vakirtzi).

of exotic material was not restricted for funerary deposition as was the case of the spindles of Kalyvia near Phaistos and Perati in Attica (see Sections 3.4.1–2), but were also used in domestic contexts.

In the southeast Aegean, significant Mycenaean influence has been noted in Rhodes in the Dodecanese. Although this is mostly represented by cemeteries and burial sites (Benzi 1988), rescue excavations have revealed facets of everyday life at Mycenaean Ialysos (Marketou 2010, 785–786). Loomweights of the Cretan, discoid type continued to be used on the warp-weighted loom in this period, following the earlier introduction of Cretan weaving technology on the island during the MBA period (Marketou 2009, see Section 3.3.2). At Ialysos, twenty-one loomweights were found on the floor of a room near a kiln, in an arrangement that implies that this space was abandoned while the loom was still set-up. Moreover, the excavator associated the kiln with the manufacture and firing of the loomweights (Marketou 2004).

3.4.3 The Mainland, LH IIIA-C

Textile Tools and Production Facilities

In the heart of the Mycenaean world in the northeastern Peloponnese, at the peak of the palatial era during the LH IIIA-B periods, thread manufacture took place both at palatial and non-palatial sites, judging from the spindle whorl assemblages. In most cases where metric data have been made available, those reveal a wide range of spindle whorl sizes. Very small whorls weighing less than 10 gr are well represented, indicating that some of the production was orientated to very fine thread (Andersson Strand and Nosch 2015, passim). Spindle whorls made of clay or stone, including small 'conuli', are widespread in Mycenae, Tiryns, Midea, Asine, Pylos, and Nichoria, to name some of the sites with published textile tools assemblages (Carington Smith 1975, 418–457; Carington Smith 1992; Rahmstorf 2008, 17–59; Andersson Strand and Nosch 2015, passim).

All of these sites document a long and complicated history of building, destructions, and rebuilding, as well as a long history of excavation campaigns, making the distinction of closed contexts, and the clarification of textile craft spaces, challenging. In the case of Mycenae in the Argolid, the seat of the Mycenaean state, Tournavitou et al. (2015, 255) warn against underestimating the taphonomic, stratigraphic, and architectural complexities of the site, when studying potential evidence of thread manufacture and weaving. Identifying spaces of textile craft is difficult, given that many excavated areas remain unpublished. Nonetheless, the analysis of a sample of textile tools found at Mycenae (Tournavitou et al. 2015) has highlighted the frequency of stone spindle whorls both on the Citadel and in the Lower Town. In the Citadel, hundreds of steatite 'conuli' have been recovered, but only a few from closely dated contexts. One 'conuli' group originating from the Shrine with the Frescoes is described as part of a votive assemblage (Tournavitou et al. 2015, 259). Although these objects are often rejected as spindle whorls, their identification as such cannot be completely ruled out (see earlier, Section 3.3.3). This is the second case of textile tools having been found in a Mycenaean shrine, following that of Phylakopi on Melos (see Section 3.4.3). In the Lower Town of Mycenae, domestic spinning activities have been identified in the case of the House of the Oil Merchant and House I of the Panagia Houses. Although whorls were also recovered in many other spaces, the contextual analysis of buildings and their contents does not always support the identification of textile production loci (Tournavitou et al. 2015, 257–259).

In contrast to spindle whorls, loomweights in LH IIIA and IIIB deposits in Mycenaean Peloponnesian sites are scarce. Only a few loomweights that are variations of the Cretan discoid type are reported from Mycenae (Carington Smith 1992, 689), from Tiryns, along with examples of the torus-shaped type (Rahmstorf 2008, 53), from the palatial complex of Pylos and from Nichoria (Carington Smith 1975, 448, 450; 1992, 687). In the case of Pylos, loomweights of the rectangular type, like those used at Kastri on Kythera (Cutler 2021, 242) were found in the Wine Magazine of the palace, a space unlikely to have been used for weaving (Cutler 2021, 242). The rarity of loomweights suggests that weaving with the warp-weighted loom in the LH IIIA–B Peloponnese was likely limited in scale. Another type of textile tool that occurs in the region during this period, the so-called 'pin beater', perhaps indicates the use of a different type of loom: 'pin beaters' are considered as an accessory for tapestry weaving (Smith 2012), a technique that was performed on the vertical two-beam loom in 18th Dynasty Egypt (Barber 1991, 158). Given the documentation of tapestry-woven cloth in Myceanae (Spantidaki 2022), it is worth considering the possibility that the scarcity of loomweights and the presence of 'pin beaters' point to the use of the two-beam loom in this region as well.

At Mycenaean Kadmeia (Thebes), Boeotia, a similar picture emerges, based on the exploration of plots in the modern town (Alberti et al. 2015). Insofar the Mycenaean deposits could be uncovered mainly through rescue excavations, textile tools from LH IIIB contexts are limited to spindle whorls made of stone and clay, as well as stone 'conuli'. Weaving is indicated primarily by unpierced clay spools that were recovered from LH IIIB2 deposits (Alberti et al. 2015, 288–290) while other types of loomweights are scarce. It is likely that Mycenaean Kadmeia was the centre of a wool industry, as wool administration is attested in the records of the Linear B archive discovered in Thebes. This has led some scholars to identify wool processing and storage areas, including probable wool-washing facilities in the Mycenaean horizon as well (Alberti et al. 2015, 286).

In Athens, Attica, the excavation of a Mycenaean site at Kontopigado, Alimos, revealed features that indicate an industrial installation. The site, abandoned before the LH IIIC period, consists of parallel, elongated channels 30–60 m long, and several pits, all dug in the natural bedrock, as well as three wells, indicating a water regulation system. Although no textile tools or organic remains related to such use have been reported, the excavators identified the site as a facility for the processing of flax (Kaza-Papageorgiou 2011): flax needs to lie in water for about 15 days so that the woody parts of the plant rot, making it easier to extract the fibres from the stem (Barber 1991, 13).

The weaving technological landscape of the LH IIIC period is marked by the widespread occurrence of the unpierced clay spool type (Figure 26), as was also the case in Crete. At Mycenae, a group of thirty-five spools were found in the East Basement of the LH IIIC building defined as the Granary that was destroyed by fire (Wace et al. 1921–1923, 54), along with spindle whorls made of stone and clay, as well as a 'small piece of carbonized canvas' (Wace et al. 1921–1923, 55, see further, *Excavated Textiles*). A group of spools was also found in the large Room XLIV of House I in LH III Asine (Frödin and Persson 1938, 78, 309, Fig. 213). At Tiryns, more than one hundred spools were recovered from well-stratified, late-LH IIIC contexts in the Lower Acropolis (Rahmstorf 2008, 59–61). These tools also have a strong representation in LH IIIC Lefkandi, on Euboea, where more than three hundred, made of unfired clay, have been found, along with a much smaller group of seven ring-shaped clay artefacts, perhaps also loomweights, and less than fifty clay spindle whorls (Evely 2006, 296–300).

These spools have a wide range of sizes, but on average they are much lighter than other types of Bronze Age loomweights. Whether used for weaving on the warp-weighted loom or for the technique of narrow band weaving envisaged by E. Barber (1997), they would work well with fine types of thread. The small spindle whorls attested in LH IIIA-C deposits are compatible with these production targets. Spinning fine thread requires great skill, and it is possible that craftspeople who were able to produce these yarns were enjoying special status in their communities. Perhaps an indication of this status is exemplified by the deposition of spindles in graves. In the case of Perati, East Attica, where a large LH IIIC cemetery was found, the excavator reported that three female tombs were furnished with 'at least five spindles' (Iakovidis 1970, 350–354). One of these, made of ivory, was preserved intact and gives us a good idea of how these tools would have looked like (Figure 28). These ivory spindles would have

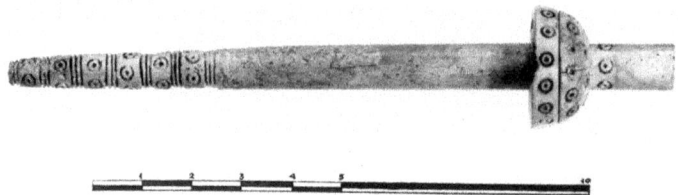

Figure 28 Ivory spindle with spindle whorl from the cemetery of Perati, Attica (image reproduced from Iakovidis 1969, Pl. 15: Δ211 ©The Athens Archaeological Society).

certainly stood out as spinning implements, at least compared to the simpler, wooden ones equipped with clay whorls. However, a different opinion was expressed by Murray (2018) who suggested that exotic items used as funerary offerings at Perati were not necessarily elite markers but may instead be symptoms of the extremely diverse burial customs that can be observed in this LH IIIC cemetery.

Excavated Textiles and Imprints

Evidence of textile craft deriving from extant textiles or textile imprints from the LH III southern Mainland is rare. A few lumps of clay from the interior of Tomb XXI at the cemetery of Deiras, Argos, dated to LHIIIA2-IIIB, preserve cloth imprints (Siennicka 2025). The 'canvas' found in LH IIIC deposits in the Granary at Mycenae mentioned earlier has yet to be re-examined.

The end of the Aegean Bronze Age features the best preserved and most sophisticated textile corpus found in Greece up to date. The excavation of a tumulus at the site of Toumba, Lefkandi, Euboea, revealed the rich burial of a man and a woman (Popham et al. 1982). The cremated remains of the male burial were found in a bronze amphora imported from Cyprus and dated to the Late Bronze Age (Catling 1993). Within the amphora, several textiles were found in a good state of preservation, including an almost complete (main) garment (Figure 29a), two textile fragments, and two narrow bands (Margariti and Spantidaki 2020).

Given the dating of the burial site of Toumba to the Protogeometric period, the textiles were previously considered to reflect Iron Age textile craft (Barber 1991, 197). However, recent radiocarbon dating yielded absolute dates between the late thirteenth to late eleventh centuries BCE for the main garment and one of the other two textile fragments, and a range between the thirteenth and the tenth centuries BCE for the third textile (Margariti and Spantidaki 2020, 403,

Table 2, 410). It is possible, then, that at least some of the cloth items were Late Bronze Age heirlooms.

The Lefkandi textiles have been recently re-examined, and the results were published in a comprehensive article (Margariti and Spantidaki 2020). After conservation, the main garment (Margariti and Spantidaki 2020, 'Textile 1') was restored as a feet-long garment with an opening for the neck but no sleeves openings (Margariti and Spantidaki 2020, 402). The ground weave is plain balanced (Table 2), while the upper part of the garment (Figure 29b) corresponding roughly to the torso area, has additional knotted pile weave with symmetrical knots (Margariti and Spantidaki 2020, 403–405). This weave is created with supplementary weft threads twining around two successive warp threads, to create small loops or knots that are left hanging to form a pile surface (Emery 1966, 221; Barber 1991, 201–202, Fig. 7.10). As to the materials used for these textiles, flax was used in most cases. However, 'Textile 3', described as a 'very fine weft-faced tabby', with a thread count of 20x80 threads per sq. cm, is suggested to have been made of wool (Barber 1991, 410). The narrow bands, manufactured of linen threads, possibly combined with woollen ones, bear geometric patterns such as chevrons and zig-zag designs, created through the weaving of double warps, wefts and probably additional threads (decorative warps?) that are today lost (Barber 1991, 405–406).

The textiles of Lefkandi preserve an extraordinary variety of weaves and decorative techniques, including plain weave, knotted pile, weft-wrapping, and tapestry, while testifying to the use of various thread types in each cloth piece, as well as the use of different coloured threads, some of which are dyed in purple (Barber 1991, 403). These textiles thus correspond to a level of craftsmanship and creativity that echoes the degree of textile specialization that had been achieved during the peak of the Mycenaean period, at least two centuries earlier, as conveyed in the Linear B documents (Killen 2007). The textile-related records include numerous terms that refer to various colours and textures as well as terms that reflect the elaboration and finishing of the cloth. Some of the professional designations on the Pylos tablets convey specializations such as spinners (Figure 30), decorators of cloth, seamstresses, and *o-nu-ke*-makers (Killen 2007, 55; Del Freo et al. 2010, 345), while terms on the Knossos tablets refer to blue, red, brown, grey, purple-coloured textiles, as well as to cloth with multicoloured *o-nu-ke* (Rougemont 2014, 355–356). The term *o-nu-ke* has been understood as 'fringes' by some scholars, and as some sort of 'added decoration' by others (Nosch 2014, 387).

Could the Lefkandi textiles be considered as one of the latest examples of the achievements of palatial weaving workshops? The radiocarbon dating of the textiles to the period between the thirteenth and the tenth centuries allows the contemplation of such a scenario, especially given the presence of another

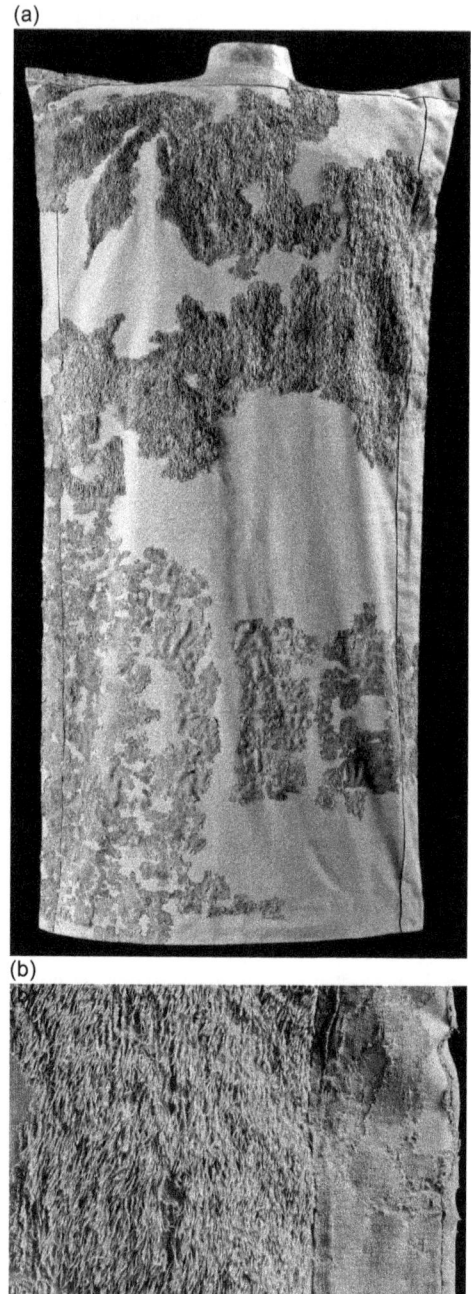

Figure 29a The main garment of Lefkandi (©The New Archaeological Museum of Chalkis/ Socratis Mavromatis/ODAP/Hellenic Ministry of Culture).
b Knotted pile weave, detail of the main garment of Lefkandi (©The New Archaeological Museum of Chalkis/ Socratis Mavromatis/ODAP/Hellenic Ministry of Culture).

Figure 30 Clay tablet from Pylos (PY Aa240) with a Linear B inscription recording spinning women (©Hellenic National Archaeological Museum/ODAP/Hellenic Ministry of Culture).

heirloom, the bronze amphora that contained the cloth items, dated to the thirteenth to twelfth centuries BCE (Catling 1993, 87). The amphora, however, is an import from Cyprus. The possibility that the textiles were also imported, perhaps from Cyprus as well, should not be ruled out, given LH IIIC Lefkandi's involvement in short and long-distance trade (Sherratt 2006, 308–309).

4 Overview of Aegean Bronze Age Textile Craft

Variety, technical diversity, and creativity characterize the textile history of the Aegean region in the 2,000 years encompassing the Bronze Age. The beginning of the period does not herald the start of sophisticated textile production. It is simply the 'next moment' in a long trajectory of craftsmanship. Both the thread manufacturing technology and the weaving techniques of the Early Bronze Age draw from considerably older traditions. The spindle and the vertical warp-weighted loom are technologies that date at least as early as the Middle Neolithic (Carington Smith 1975). The same is true for fibre economy and fibre technology. It is likely that Bronze Age textile craft relied on a range of textile fibres, perhaps including wild silk as well as nettle. Practices of gathering textile fibres from 'wild' or non-domesticated species, apparently drawing from pre-Neolithic traditions that survived into the Neolithic (Rast-Eicher et al. 2021; Bender Jørgensen et al. 2023), probably continued in the Bronze Age and coexisted with the practice of harvesting fibre from domesticated species, that resulted in the standardized wool and flax economies of the third and second millennia BCE.

Within the third millennium BCE, advanced technological know-how in thread manufacture can be surmised. The assemblages of spinning tools studied from various sites in the Aegean and Mainland Greece reveal the diversified production of a range of different thread qualities, from very fine to coarse. The scant evidence for actual textiles emerging from imprints and mineralized, carbonized and calcified fragments, showcase the need for the simultaneous use of various thread qualities in the same cloth, for wefts, warps and supplementary decorative, strengthening or 'sewing' threads. Textile production in the Early Bronze Age was domestic but sophisticated. Cloth was essential in every aspect of life, from dress for the human body, to more 'technical uses', judging from the impressions of textiles on ceramic artefacts and the imprints on clay sealings. Such 'technical uses' did not entail only coarse cloth qualities. The few extant textiles and their imprints suggest that the investment in time, effort, and resources for fine products was not intended exclusively for clothing the human body. Fine cloth was also used for 'dressing' non-human 'bodies', as the metal dagger from the Amorgos tomb seems to suggest. Does this indicate a widespread availability of finely woven cloth?

One notable achievement in the textile craft of the second millennium BCE appears to have been on the level of elaboration and cloth decoration. This was apparently achieved with appliqués, non-textile elements such as beads and metal ornaments (Konstantinidi-Syvridi 2014), but also on a purely textile level, with an investment in creating colourful patterning with dyed yarns, and thread decorative techniques such as looping, knotting and tassel-making. The production of dyes for multicoloured textiles became so important that it evolved into a centrally managed industry on Crete, as indicated by the facilities for dye production. In the corpus of excavated textiles, colour is barely traceable, but thanks to figurative art, primarily the art of second-millennium frescoes, it is possible to grasp the rich colour palette at the disposal of weavers. Textile polychromy must have developed in parallel to wool economy, since wool absorbs dyes much better than bast fibres.

The use of supplementary threads in the ground weave for the decoration of cloth with an array of additional thread structures is another important breakthrough of Aegean textile craft during the Bronze Age. 'Tangible' evidence of these techniques was encountered for the first time with the discovery of the Akrotiri textiles. It is impressive that the supplementary threads, the knots, the tassels, and the traces of embroidery were observed on miniscule, carbonized cloth fragments. This fact demonstrates the importance of analysing even the smallest scraps of textile finds, and reinforces the hope that even fragments that appear as worn-out and desperate remains at first glance may retain invaluable testimonies of textile history.

The economic and symbolic significance of textiles is underlined by the flourishing of weaving workshops across the Aegean. Textile industries were being established in urban centres in Crete, at important harbour towns of the insular Aegean and in surrounding coastal areas from the early second millennium BCE. Interestingly, the coastal and insular weaving centres that emerged outside of Crete were equipped with Cretan-type warp-weighted looms. However, as the evidence shows, the diffusion of the Cretan weaving technology at its earliest moment, should be understood as a specifically Knossian effect. The weaving technological landscape on Protopalatial Crete is far from homogeneous, and on Crete itself there was no one, specific type of 'Minoan loomweight'. Malia provides us with 'hoards' of spherical loomweights from Protopalatial contexts, standing in contrast to Knossos in terms of the production targets: fine and densely woven, perhaps even patterned textiles were produced at the latter, while open, or weft-faced fabrics at the former. The islanders who adopted 'Cretan ways of weaving' in the early second millennium BCE were following the example of Knossos. But then Knossos itself, in its Neopalatial phase, followed the example of other Protopalatial centres, perhaps most importantly Malia, as weavers based around the Knossian palatial complex were now equipping their looms with spherical loomweights. The types of fabrics produced at Knossos were also produced in Archanes and several other locations in north-central Crete. In the islands, however, the Knossian shift to spherical loomweights does not appear to have had an effect. In the Cyclades, the Southeast Aegean and even the North Aegean, weaving continued 'as usual', with discoid loomweights, suitable to produce dense, fine, and probably balanced weaves. The only exception is Akrotiri, where along with the dominant discoid loomweights, a few examples of spherical loomweights were found scattered in the LC town. Their occurrence indicates an attempt to engage with the weaving of open or weft-faced textiles following, again, the example of Knossos, and a few other places such as Archanes. Perhaps the Theran weavers had just began weaving a new type of fabric, but there was just not enough time to upscale this production before Akrotiri was abandoned and destroyed by the volcanic eruption.

Mycenaean textile production emerges as an extremely sophisticated sector of the political economy of Mycenaean states, while the textual sources convey a highly specialized industry. However, the documentary evidence does not correspond well with the archaeological record. In terms of textile remains the record is very poor, while the material remains of textile technology document more clearly the stage of spinning thread than the stage of weaving cloth. One of the most poignant emerging patterns, however, regards the association of textile craft and religious practices. The deposition of textile tools in shrines, attested in Mycenae and in Phylakopi, perhaps should be considered related to the ritual offering of cloth (Boloti 2009). On the Mainland, yarn production is quite visible archaeologically, but the weaving technology is elusive, at least in the major centres. Whether this implies a geographical division of labour or an archaeologically invisible weaving technology remains an open question. What is important to note, however, is that the Mycenaean administration of the textile industry at Final Palatial Knossos did not bring about any significant change in the local, weaving technology: the spherical loomweights that dominate in LM II contexts, as they also did in the Neopalatial phase, testify as much. However, change is observed towards the end of the Late Bronze Age, when a new type of loomweight, the unpierced clay spool, appears to spread across the Aegean. Does this tool imply a fashion for colourful narrow bands, created efficiently with these portable weaving implements, wherever one travelled, as E. Barber suggested? And if so, would this technology add to the pattern of weavers travelling around the Aegean and the Eastern Mediterranean, where these spools are also very common (Rahmstorf 2008)?

The end of the Bronze Age did not signify an end for textiles, despite the collapse of the Mycenaean palatial infrastructure that had in many ways supported and advanced textile craftsmanship. The garment of Lefkandi, dated between the thirteenth and the eleventh century BCE, indicates that high-quality cloth was still in demand during this time of severe political and economic destabilization. Moreover, the safeguarding of Late Bronze Age textile heirlooms and their disposition in an Iron Age prestige burial showcases the participation of textiles in strategies of monumentalization and memory making.

5 Conclusion

Although we will likely never fully recover the complete range of techniques, textures, colours, scents, sounds, appearances, and uses of Aegean Bronze Age textiles, the emergence of Textile Archaeology as a dynamic research field in recent decades offers imaginative and innovative approaches to analysing and understanding the material remains of textile production and consumption. A substantial body of new data is being generated through advanced analytical methodologies that focus on the technical aspects of textile material culture. This growing body of evidence invites a critical reassessment of earlier assumptions, hypotheses, and interpretive models concerning Aegean textile craft.

At the same time, current research has the potential to reveal how textiles, by clothing both human and non-human bodies, functioned as active agents of social and economic transformation. The Bronze Age was a period marked by expanding regional and interregional networks among Aegean communities and those in surrounding areas. Textiles likely served as a 'second skin' for individuals migrating, whether voluntarily or forcibly, or simply travelling across the Aegean and the Eastern Mediterranean, bringing diverse cloth cultures into contact.

As textile production became increasingly central to political economies, cloth and garments were progressively integrated into systems of exchange, including gift-giving, trade, and other forms of transaction. The intensifying, multidirectional flow of people, goods, and ideas throughout the Bronze Age suggests that textile craftsmanship was a widely interconnected and collaboratively shaped domain of human creativity. It was rich in variation, material expression, and deeply embedded in the enduring maritime networks that defined Bronze Age connectivity.

References

Alberti, L. (2012). Making Visible the Invisible: Cretan Objects Mentioned in the Cuneiform Texts of Mari and Archaeological Discoveries in Crete in the II Millennium BC. *Studi Micenei ed Egeo-Anatolici* **54**, 117–142.

Alberti, M. E. (2007). Washing and Dyeing Installations of the Ancient Mediterranean: Towards a Definition from Roman Times Back to Minoan Crete. In C. Gillis and M.-L. Nosch, eds., *Ancient Textiles. Production, Craft and Society*, Oxford: Oxbow Books, pp. 59–63.

Alberti, M. E., Aravantinos, V., Fappas, I., et al. (2015). Textile Tools from Thebes, Mainland Greece. In E. Andersson Strand and M.-L. Nosch, eds., *Tools, Textiles and Contexts. Investigating Textile Production in the Aegean and Eastern Mediterranean Bronze Age*, Oxford: Oxbow Books, pp. 279–292.

Alexopoulos, G. (2021). The Gold and the Red: Approaching the Invisible at Akrotiri, Thera. In C. C. Doumas and A. Devetzi, eds., *Akrotiri, Thera. Forty Years of Research (1967–2007). Scientific Colloquium, Athens, 15–16 December 2007*, Athens: Society for the Promotion of Studies on Prehistoric Thera, pp. 491–513.

Andersson Strand, E. (2015a). The Basics of Textile Tools and Textile Technology-from Fibre to Fabric. In E. Andersson Strand and M.-L. Nosch, eds., *Tools, Textiles and Contexts: Investigating Textile Production in the Aegean and Eastern Mediterranean Bronze Age*, Oxford: Oxbow Books, pp. 39–60.

Andersson Strand, E. (2015b). From Tools to Textiles, Concluding Remarks. In E. Andersson Strand and M.-L. Nosch, eds., *Tools, Textiles and Contexts: Investigating Textile Production in the Aegean and Eastern Mediterranean Bronze Age*, Oxford: Oxbow Books, pp. 139–151.

Andersson Strand, E. and Nosch, M.-L., eds. (2015). *Tools, Textiles and Contexts: Investigating Textile Production in the Aegean and Eastern Mediterranean Bronze Age*, Oxford: Oxbow Books.

Andersson Strand, E., Mannering, U. and Nosch, M.-L. (2022). Old Textiles – New Possibilities. Ten Years on. In A. Ulanowska, K. Grömer, I. Vanden Berghe and M. Öhrman, eds., *Ancient Textile Production from an Interdisciplinary Perspective*, Cham: Springer, pp. 19–35.

Apostolakou, V., Brogan, T. M. and Betancourt, P. P. (2020). *Alatzomouri Pefka: A Middle Minoan IIB Workshop Making Organic Dyes*, Philadelphia: Instap Academic Press.

References

Aruz, J. (2008). *Marks of Distinction. Seals and Cultural Exchange between the Aegean and the Orient*, CMS Beih. 7, Mainz: Philipp von Zabern.

Balfanz, K. (1995). Bronzezeitliche Spinnwirtel aus Troia. *Studia Troica* **5**, 117–144.

Banks, E. (1967). *The Early and Middle Helladic Small Objects from Lerna*, Ann Arbor: University of Michigan.

Barber, E. J. W. (1991). *Prehistoric Textiles*, Princeton: Princeton University Press.

Barber, E. J. W. (1997). Minoan Women and the Challenges of Weaving for Home, Trade, and Shrine. In R. Laffineur and P. Betancourt, eds., *TEXNH: Craftsmen, Craftswomen and Craftsmanship in the Aegean Bronze Age. Proceedings of the 6th International Aegean Conference, Philadelphia, Temple University, 18–21 April 1996*, Liège: Université de Liège and University of Texas at Austin, pp. 515–519.

Barber, E. J. W. (2016). Minoans, Mycenaeans, and Keftiu (with a New Introduction). In M. C. Shaw and A. P. Chapin, eds., *Woven Threads: Patterned Textiles of the Aegean Bronze Age*. Oxford: Oxbow Books, pp. 205–237.

Bender Jørgensen, L., Rast-Eicher, A. and Wendrich, W. (2023). Earliest Evidence for Textile Technologies. *Paléorient* **49(1)**, 213–228.

Bennet, J. (2024). Geography. In J. Killen, ed., *The New Documents in Mycenaean Greek. Volume One. Introductory Essays. Drawings of Selected Tablets*, Vol. 1, Cambridge: Cambridge University Press, pp. 255–266.

Benzi, M. (1988). Mycenaean Rhodes: A Summary. In S. Dietz and I. Papachristodoulou, eds., *Archaeology in the Dodecanese*, Copenhagen: The National Museum of Denmark, Department of Near Eastern and Classical Antiquities, pp. 59–72.

Bernabò Brea, L. (1964). *Poliochni: Citta preistorica Nell'Isola di Lemnos, Vol. I. 1–2*, Roma: L'Erma.

Bernabò Brea, L. (1976). *Poliochni: Citta preistorica Nell'Isola di Lemnos, Vol. II. 1–2*, Roma: L'Erma.

Betancourt, P. P. (2007). Textile Production at Pseira; the Knotted Net. In C. Gillis and M.-L. Nosch, eds., *Ancient Textiles: Production, Craft and Society*, Oxford: Oxbow Books, pp. 185–189.

Birtacha, K. (2008). 'Cooking' Installations in LC IA Akrotiri on Thera: A Preliminary Study of the 'Kitchen' in Pillar Shaft 65. In N. J. Brodie, J. Doole, G. Gavalas and C. Renfrew, eds., *Horizon: A Colloquium on the Prehistory of the Cyclades, Cambridge, 25th–28th March 2004*, Cambridge: McDonald Institute for Archaeological Research, pp. 389–416.

Birtacha, K., Sotiropoulou, S., Perdikatsis, V. and Apostolaki, Ch. (2021). Pigments: New Data on the Materials, their Processing and their Use in the Prehistoric Settlement at Akrotiri. In C. C. Doumas and A. Devetzi, eds., *Akrotiri, Thera: Forty Years of Research (1967–2007). Scientific Colloquium, Athens, 15–16 December 2007*, Athens: Society for the Promotion of Studies on Prehistoric Thera, pp. 195–214.

Blakolmer, F. (2010). The Iconography of the Shaft Grave Period as Evidence for a Middle Helladic Tradition of Figurative Arts? In A. Philippa-Touchais, G. Touchais, S. Voutsaki and J. Wright, eds., *Mesohelladika: The Greek Mainland in the Middle Bronze Age*, BCH Supplément 52, Athènes: École Française d'Athènes, pp. 509–519.

Blakolmer, F. (2018). A 'Special Procession' in Minoan Seal Images: Observations on Ritual Dress in Minoan Crete. In P. Pavúk, V. Klontza-Jaklová and Anthony Harding, eds., *ΕΥΔΑΙΜΩΝ: Studies in honour of Jan Bouzek*, Prague: Faculty of Arts, Charles University, pp. 29–50.

Boloti, T. (2009). Ritual Offering of Textiles and Garments in the Late Bronze Age Aegean. *Arachne* **3**, 52–79.

Boloti, T. (2014). *e-ri-ta*'s Dress: Contribution to the Study of the Mycenaean Priestesses' Attire. In M. Harlow, C. Michel and M.-L. Nosch, eds., *Prehistoric, Ancient near Eastern and Aegean Textiles and Dress: An Interdisciplinary Anthology*, Oxford: Oxbow Books, pp. 245–270.

Boulotis, C. (2008). Les nouveaux documents en linéaire A d'Akrotiri (Théra): remarques préliminaires. *Bulletin de Correspondance Hellénique* **122**, 407–411.

Brogan, T., Betancourt, P. P. and Apostolakou, V. (2012). The Purple Dye Industry of Eastern Crete. In M.-L. Nosch and R. Laffineur, eds., *KOSMOS. Jewellery, Adornment and Textiles in the Aegean Bronze Age. Proceedings of the 13th International Aegean Conference, University of Copenhagen, Danish National Research Foundation's Centre for Textile Research, 21–26 April 2010*, Leuven-Liège: Peeters, pp. 187–192.

Broodbank, C. (2013). *The Making of the Middle Sea: A History of the Mediterranean from the Beginning to the Emergence of the Classical World*, London: Oxford University Press.

Bruun-Lundgren, M., Andersson Strand, E. and Hallager, B. P. (2015). Textile Tools from Khania, Crete, Greece. In E. Andersson Strand and M.-L. Nosch, eds., *Tools, Textiles and Contexts: Investigating Textile Production in the Aegean and Eastern Mediterranean Bronze Age*, Oxford: Oxbow Books, pp. 197–206.

Burke, B. (2003). The Spherical Loomweights. In P. A. Mountjoy, ed., *Knossos: The South House*, Supplementary Volume 34, London: The British School at Athens, pp. 195–197.

Burke, B. (2005). Materialization of Mycenaean Ideology and the Ayia Triada Sarcophagus. *American Journal of Archaeology* **109**, 403–422.

Burke, B. (2010). *From Minos to Midas: Ancient Cloth Production in the Aegean and in Anatolia*, Oxford: Oxbow Books.

Burke, B. (2012). Looking for Sea-Silk in the Bronze Age Aegean. In M.-L. Nosch and R. Laffineur, eds., *KOSMOS. Jewellery, Adornment and Textiles in the Aegean Bronze Age. Proceedings of the 13th International Aegean Conference, University of Copenhagen, Danish National Research Foundation's Centre for Textile Research, 21–26 April 2010*, Leuven-Liège: Peeters, pp. 171–176.

Burke, B. and Dimova, B. (2023). Cloth for the Dead at Ancient Eleon in Central Greece. In H. Frielinghaus, J. Stroszeck and A. Sieverling, eds., *Textilien im antiken Griechenland: Ein Beitrag zur Potential-Evaluierung*, Möhnesse: Bibliopolis, pp. 11–20.

Carington Smith, J. (1975). *Spinning, Weaving and Textile Manufacture in Prehistoric Greece, from the Beginning of the Neolithic to the End of the Mycenaean Ages; with Particular Reference to the Evidence found on Archaeological Excavations*, Unpublished PhD thesis, University of Tasmania.

Carington Smith, J. (1977). Appendix 2: Cloth and Mat Impressions. In J. E. Coleman, ed., *Kephala: A Late Neolithic Settlement and Cemetery. Keos Volume I*, Princeton: American School of Classical Studies, pp. 114–127.

Carington Smith, J. (1992). Spinning and Weaving Equipment. In W. A. Macdonald and N. C. Wilkie, eds., *Excavations at Nichoria in Southwestern Greece. 2. The Bronze Age Occupation*, Minneapolis: University of Minnesota Press, pp. 674–711.

Catling, H. W. (1993). The Bronze Amphora and Burial Urn. In M. R. Popham, P. G. Calligas and L. H. Sackett, eds., *Lefkandi II. The Protogeometric Building at Toumba. Part 2. The Excavation, Architeccture and Finds*, London: The British School at Athens, pp. 81–97.

Cherry, J. F. and Davis, J. L. (2007). The Other Finds. In C. Renfrew, N. Brodie, C. Morris and C. Scarre, eds., *Excavations at Phylakopi in Melos 1974–1977*, Supplementary Volume 42, London: The British School at Athens, pp. 401–464.

Cline, E. (1994). *Sailing the Wine-Dark Sea: International Trade and the Late Bronze Age Aegean*, BAR International Series 591. Oxford: British Archaeological Reports.

Crouwel, J., Prent, M. and Shipley, D. G. J. (2007). Geraki: An Acropolis Site in Lakonia: Preliminary Report on the Thirteenth Season. *Pharos* **15**, 1–16.

Crowley, J. L. (2008). Mycenaean Art and Architecture. In C. W. Shelmerdine, ed., *The Cambridge Companion to the Aegean Bronze Age*, New York: Cambridge University Press, pp. 258–288.

Crowley, J. L. (2012). Prestige Clothing in the Bronze Age Aegean. In M.-L. Nosch and R. Laffineur, eds., *KOSMOS. Jewellery, Adornment and Textiles in the Aegean Bronze Age. Proceedings of the 13th International Aegean Conference, University of Copenhagen, Danish National Research Foundation's Centre for Textile Research, 21–26 April 2010*, Leuven-Liège: Peeters, pp. 231–239.

Cummer, W. W. and Schofield, E. (1984). *Keos III. Ayia Irini: House A*, Mainz on Rhine: Philipp von Zabern.

Cutler, J. E. (2016a). Fashioning Identity: Weaving Technology, Dress and Cultural Change in the Middle and Late Bronze Age Southern Aegean. In E. Gorogianni, P. Pavúk and L. Girella, eds., *Beyond Thalassocracies: Understanding Processes of Minoanisation and Mycenaeanisation in the Aegean*, Oxford: Oxbow Books, pp. 172–185.

Cutler, J. E. (2016b). Producing Textiles: The Evidence from the Textile Tools. In M. Tsipopoulou, ed., *Petras, Siteia I. A Minoan Palatial Settlement in Eastern Crete. Excavation of Houses I.1 and I.2*, Philadelphia: Instap Academic Press, pp. 175–184.

Cutler, J. E. (2021). *Crafting Minoanisation: Textiles, Crafts Production and Social Dynamics in the Bronze Age Southern Aegean*, Oxford: Oxbow Books.

Cutler, J., Andersson Strand, E. and Nosch, M.-L. (2013). Textile Production in Quartier Mu. In J. C. Poursat, ed., *Le Quartier Mu V*, Études Crétoises 34, Athens: École Française d'Athènes, pp. 95–119.

Cutler, J., Whitelaw, T. and Gleba, M. (2024). The Weaving Equipment. In R. N. L. Barber, ed., *Phylakopi, Melos, 1896–99: The Finds in the National Archaeological Museum, Athens, Vol. 2,* Supplementary Volume *53*, London: The British School at Athens, pp. 701–739.

Davis, J. (1984). Cultural Innovation and the Minoan Thalassocracy at Ayia Irini, Keos. In R. Hagg and N. Marinatos, eds., *The Minoan Thalassocracy: Myth and Reality. Proceedings of the Third International Symposium at the Swedish Institute in Athens, 31 May-5 June 1982*, Stockholm: Paul Åstroms Förlag, pp. 159–165.

Davis, J. L. and Stocker, S. R. (2016). The Lord of the Gold Rings: The Griffin Warrior of Pylos. *Hesperia* **85(4)**, 627–655.

Del Freo, M., Nosch, M.-L. and Rougemont, F. (2010). The Terminology of Textiles in the Linear B Tablets, Including Some Considerations on Linear A Logograms and Abbreviations. In C. Michel and M.-L. Nosch, eds., *Textile Terminologies in the Ancient near East and Mediterranean from the Third to the First Millennia BC*, Oxford: Oxbow Books, pp. 338–373.

Devetzi, A. (2014). Λίθινα εργαλεία και σκεύη. In A. Angelopoulou, ed., *Κορφάρι των Αμυγδαλιών (Πάνορμος) Νάξου*, Athens: Archaeological Receipts Fund, pp. 301–451.

Doumas, C. (1977). *Early Bronze Age Burial Habits in the Cyclades*, Jonsered: Paul Åstroms Förlag.

Doumas, C. (1992). *The Wall-Paintings of Thera*, Athens: The Thera Foundation/P. M. Nomikos.

Doumas, C. (2008). Chambers of Mystery. In N. J. Brodie, J. Doole, G. Gavalas and C. Renfrew, eds., *Horizon: A Colloquium on the Prehistory of the Cyclades, Cambridge, 25th–28th March 2004*, Cambridge: McDonald Institute for Archaeological Research, pp. 165–175.

Doumas, C. (2018). The Human Figure at the Mercy of the Paintbrush. In A. G. Vlachopoulos, ed., *Paintbrushes: Wall-Painting and Vase-Painting of the Second Millennium BC in Dialogue*, Athens: University of Ioannina/ Hellenic Ministry of Culture and Sports, pp. 27–41.

Doumas, C. (2019). Ανασκαφή Ακρωτηρίου Θήρας. *PAE* (2019), 287–300.

Doumas, C. (2021). Forty Years of Research. In C. C. Doumas and A. Devetzi, eds., *Akrotiri, Thera: Forty Years of Research (1967–2007). Scientific Colloquium, Athens, 15–16 December 2007*, Athens: Society for the Promotion of Studies on Prehistoric Thera, pp. 13–31.

Douny, E. (2013). Wild Silk Textiles from the Dogon of Mali: The Production, Material Efficacy and Cultural Significance of Sheen. *Textile* **11(1)**, 58–77.

Egan, E. (2015). Working within the Lines: Artists' Grids and Painted Floors at the Palace of Nestor. In S. Lepinski and S. McFadden, eds., *Beyond Iconography: Materials, Methods and Meaning in Ancient Surface Decoration*, Boston: Archaeological Institute of America, pp. 187–204.

Elster, E. (2003). Tools of the Spinner, Weaver, and Mat Maker. In E. Elster and C. Renfrew, eds., *Prehistoric Sitagroi: Excavations in Northeast Greece, 1968–1970. Volulme 2: The Final Report*, Los Angeles: Cotsen Institute of Archaeology at UCLA, pp. 229–282.

Elster, E., Andersson Strand, E., Nosch, M.-L. and Cutler, J. (2015). Textile Tools from Sitagroi, Northern Greece. In E. Andersson Strand and M.-L. Nosch, eds., *Tools, Textiles and Contexts: Investigating Textile*

Production in the Aegean and Eastern Mediterranean Bronze Age, Oxford: Oxbow Books, pp. 305–314.

Emery, I. (1966). *The Primary Structures of Fabrics: An Illustrated Classification*, Washington DC: The Textile Museum.

Evans, A. J. (1902). The Palace of Knossos. *Annual of the British School at Athens* **8**, 1–124.

Evans, A. (1935). *The Palace of Minos: A comparative Account of the Successive Stages of the Early Cretan Civilization as Illustrated by the Discoveries at Knossos*, Volume 4, Part 1. London: Macmillan and Co Ltd.

Evely, D. (2006). The Small Finds. In D. Evely, ed., *Lefkandi IV. The Bronze Age. The Late Helladic IIIC Settlement at Xeropolis*, BSA Supplementary Volume 39, London: The British School at Athens, pp. 265–302.

Evely, D. (2010). Crete. *Archaeological Reports, Archaeology in Greece 2009–2010* **56**, 169–201.

Evely, D. (2012). Clay Loomweights. In C. Knappett and Tim Cunningham, eds., *Palaikastro Block M. The Proto-and Neopalatial Town*. Supplementary Volume 47, London: The British School at Athens, pp. 248–252.

Ferrence, S. (2017). The Development of Clothed Figurines in Bronze Age Crete as Demonstrated by the Small Idols of Hagios Charalambos. In N. C. Stampolides and P. Sotirakopoulou, eds., *Cycladica in Crete. Cycladic and Cycladicizing figurines within their archaeological context. Proceedings of the International Symposium, Museum of Cycladic Art Athens, 1–2 October 2015*, Athens: University of Crete, pp. 537–550.

Frödin, O. and Persson, A. (1938). *Asine. Results of the Swedish Excavations 1922–1930*, Stockholm: A. Westholm.

Gavalas, G. (2013). Spindle Whorls and Related Objects. In C. Renfrew, O. Philianotou, N. Brodie, G. Gavalas, and M. Boyd, eds., *The Settlement at Dhaskalio. Volume I. The Sanctuary on Keros and the Origins of Aegean Ritual Practice: The Excavations of 2006–2008*, Cambridge: McDonald Institute for Archaeological Research, pp. 649–652.

Gavalas, G. (2018). Textile Tools and Manufacture in the Early Bronze Age Cyclades: Evidence from Amorgos and Keros. In M. Siennicka, L. Rahmstorf and A. Ulanowska, eds., *First Textiles: The Beginnings of Textile Manufacture in Europe and the Mediterranean*, Oxford: Oxbow Books, pp.175–186.

Gero, J. M. and Conkey, M. W. (1991). *Engendering Archaeology: Women and Prehistory*, Oxford: Blackwell.

Gleba, M. (2017). Tracing Textile Cultures of Italy and Greece in the early First Millennium BC. *Antiquity* **91(359)**, 1205–1222. https://doi.org/10.15184/aqy.2017.144.

Gleba, M. and Harris, S. (2019). The First Plant Bast Fibre Technology: Identifying Splicing in Archaeological Textiles. *Archaeological and Anthropological Sciences* **11**, 2329–2346.

Gorogianni, E., Cutler, J. and Fitzsimons, R. D. (2015). Something Old, Something New: Non-Local Brides as Catalysts for Cultural Exchange at Ayia Irini, Kea? In N. C. Stampolidis, C. Maner and K. Kopanias, eds., *Nostoi: Indigenous Culture, Migration and Intergration in the Aegean Islands and Western Anatolia during the Late Bronze Age and Early Iron Age*, Istanbul: Koç University Press, pp. 889–921.

Graziadio, G. (1988). The Chronology of the Graves of Circle B at Mycenae: A New Hypothesis. *American Journal of Archaeology* **92(3)**, 343–372.

Halstead, P. and Isaakidou, V. (2011). Revolutionary Secondary Products: The Development and Significance of Milking, Animal-Traction and Wool-Gathering in Later Prehistoric Europe and the Near East. In T. Wilkinson, S. Sherratt and J. Bennet, eds., *Interweaving Worlds: Systemic Interactions in Eurasia, 7th to 1st Millennia BC*, Oxford: Oxbow Books, pp. 61–76.

Hatzaki, E. (2018). Pots, Frescoes, Textiles and People: The Social Life of Decorated Pottery at Late Bronze Age Knossos and Crete. In A. G. Vlachopoulos, ed., *Paintbrushes: Wall-Painting and Vase-Painting of the Second Millennium BC in Dialogue*, Athens: University of Ioannina/Hellenic Ministry of Culture and Sports, pp. 315–327.

Iakovidis, S. (1969). *Περατή. Το νεκροταφείον. Γ΄ Πίνακες*, Athens: The Athens Archaeological Society.

Iakovidis, S. (1970). *Περατή. Το νεκροταφείον. Β΄ Γενικαί Παρατηρήσεις*, Athens: The Athens Archaeological Society.

Iakovidis, S. (1977). On the Use of Mycenaean 'Buttons'. *The Annual of the British School at Athens* **72**, 113–119.

Jones, B. R. (1998). *Minoan Women's Clothes: An Investigation of their Construction from the Depictions in Aegean art*, Ann Arbor: University of Michigan.

Jones, B. R. (2015). *Ariadne's Threads: The Construction and Significance of Clothes in the Aegean Bronze Age*, Aegaeum 38. Leuven-Liège: Peeters.

Karantzali, E. (1986). Une Tombe Minoen Récent IIIB à la Canée. *Bulletin de Correspondance Hellénique* **CX-1986,** 53–87.

Karantzali, E. (2001). *The Mycenaean Cemetery at Pylona, Rhodes*, Oxford: Archaeopress.

Karnava, A. (2018). *Seals, Sealings, and Seal Impressions from Akrotiri in Thera*, Corpus der Minoischen und Mykenischen Siegel, Beiheft 10. Heidelberg: CMS.

Karnava, A. (2019). The Inscribed Loomweight. In I. Nikolakopoulou, ed., *Akrotiri, Thera. Middle Bronze Age Pottery and Stratigraphy, Vol. I-II*, Athens: The Athens Archaeological Society, pp. 501–504.

Karo, G. (1930–1933). *Die Schactgräber von Mykenai*, Munich: Bruckmann.

Kaza-Papageorgiou, K. (2011). Κοντοπήγαδο Αλίμου Αττικής. Οικισμός των ΠΕ και ΥΕ χρόνων και ΥΕ εργαστηριακή εγκατάσταση. *Archaeologike Ephemeris* **150**, 197–274.

Kemp, B. J. and Vogelsang-Eastwood, G. (2001). *The Ancient Textile Industry at Amarna*, London: Egypt Exploration Society.

Killen, J. T. (2007). Cloth Production in Late Bronze Age Greece: the Documentary Evidence. In C. Gillis and M.-L. Nosch, eds., *Ancient Textiles. Production, Craft and Society*, Oxford: Oxbow Books, pp. 50–58.

Koh, A., Betancourt, P. P., Pareja, M. N., Brogan, T. and Apostolakou, V. (2016). Organic Residue Analysis of Pottery from the Dye Workshop at Alatsomouri-Pefka, Crete. *Journal of Archaeological Science: Reports* **7**, 536–538.

Konstantinidi-Syvridi, E. (2014). Buttons, Pins, Clips and Belts … 'Inconspicuous' Dress Accessories. In M. Harlow, C. Michel and M.-L. Nosch, eds., *Prehistoric, Ancient near Eastern and Aegean Textiles and Dress: An Interdisciplinary Anthology*, Oxford: Oxbow Books, pp. 143–157.

Lamb, W. (1928–1929/1929–1930). Excavations at Thermi in Lesbos. *The Annual of the British School at Athens* **30**, 1–52.

Lambrinoudakis, V. and P. Zafeiropoulou (1984). Ανασκαφή Πλατείας Μητροπόλεως Νάξου, *PAE* 1984, 313–339.

Lukesova, H. and Holst, B. (2024). Identifying Plant Fibres in Cultural Heritage with Optical and Electron Microscopy: How to Present Results and Avoid Pitfalls. *Heritage Science* **12(12)**, 1–14.

Maniatis, Y., Marthari, M. and Polymeris, G. S. (2023). Radiocarbon Dating of the Major Settlement at Skarkos (Ios Island, Cyclades) and Inferences for the Early Cycladic Chronology. *Radiocarbon* **65(5)**, 1057–1079.

Marangou, C. (1992). *Eidolia: figurines et miniatures du Néolithique recent et du Bronze ancien en Grèce*, BAR International Series 576, Oxford: British Archaeological Reports.

Marangou, L., Renfrew, C., Doumas, Ch., and Gavalas, G., eds. (2006). *Markiani on Amorgos: An Early Bronze Age Fortified Settlement. Overview of the Investigations 1987–1991*, Annual of the British School of Athens, Supplementary Volume 40, London: The British School at Athens.

Margariti, C. (2020). The Effects of Artificial Incomplete Burning on the Morphology and Dimensions of Cellulosic and Proteinaceous Textiles and

Fibres. *Studies in Conservation*, 1–11, https://doi.org/10.1080/00393630.2019.1709307.

Margariti, C. and Spantidaki, S. (2020). Revisiting the Hero of Lefkandi. In M. Bustamante-Álvarez, E. H. Sánchez López and Javier Jiménez Ávila, eds., *Redefining Ancient Textile Handcraft. Structures, Tools and Production Processes. Proceedings of the VIIth International Symposium on Textiles and Dyes in the Ancient Mediterranean World (Granada, Spain 2–4 October 2019)*, Purpureae Vestes VII, Granada: Universidad de Granada, pp. 401–412.

Margariti, C., Sava, G., Sava, T., Boudin, M. and Nosch, M.-L. (2023a). Radiocarbon Dating of Archaeological Textiles at Different States of Preservation. *Heritage Science*. **11**, 44.

Margariti, C. and Spantidaki, S. (2023b). Bronze Age Weaves from Thebes – A Carbonized Textile Story. In H. Frielinghaus, J. Stroszeck and A. Sieverling, eds., *Textilien im antiken Griechenland. Ein Beitrag zur Potential-Evaluierung*, Möhnesse: Bibliopolis, pp. 21–30.

Margariti, C., Lukesova, H. and Gomes, F. B. (2024). Advanced Analytical Techniques for Heritage Textiles. *Heritage Science* **12**.

Marketou, T. (2004). Μυκηναϊκός κεραμικός κλίβανος στον Προϊστορικό οικισμό της Ιαλυσού (Τριάντα, Ρόδος). In A. Kyriatsoulis, ed., *Althellenische Technologie und Technik von der prähistorischen bis zur hellenistichen Zeit mit Schwerpunk auf der prähistorischen Ephoche*, Weilheim : Verein zur Förderung der Aufarbeitung der hellenischen Geschichte, pp. 133–144.

Marketou, T. (2009). Ialysos and its Neighbouring Areas in the MBA and LB I Periods: A Chance for Peace. In C. F. Macdonald, E. Hallager and W. Dietrich-Niemeier, eds., *The Minoans in the Central, Eastern and Northern Aegean-New Evidence: Acts of a Minoan Seminar 22–23 January 2005 in Collaboration with the Danish Institute at Athens and the German Archaeological Institute at Athens*, Monographs of the Danish Institute at Athens, Vol. 8, Athens: The Danish Institute at Athens, pp. 73–96.

Marketou, T. (2010). Rhodes. In E. H. Cline, ed., *The Oxford Handbook of the Bronze Age Aegean*, New York: Oxford University Press, pp. 775–794.

Mårtensson, L., Nosch, M.-L. and Andersson Strand, E. (2009). Shape of Things: Understanding a Loom Weight. *Oxford Journal of Archaeology* **28 (4)**, 373–398.

Marthari, M. (2017). Cycladic Figurines in Settlements: The Case of the Major EC II Settlement at Skarkos on Ios and the Schematic Figurines. In M. Marthari, C. Renfrew, and M. Boyd, eds., *Early Cycladic Sculpture in Context*, Oxford: Oxbow Books, pp. 119–164.

Marthari, M. (2018). Architecture, Seals and Aspects of Social Organization in the Peak Period of the Early Bronze Age Cyclades: The Evidence from the Major Settlement at Skarkos on the Island of Ios. In H. H. Meller, D. Gronenborn, and R. Risch, eds., *Surplus without the State: Political Forms in Prehistory. 10th Archaeological Conference of Central Germany, October 19–21 2017, in Halle*, Halle: Landesamt für Denkmalpflege und Archäologie Sachsen-Anhalt, Landesmuseum für Vorgeschichte Halle, pp. 167–196.

Michaelidis, I. and Angelidis, P. (2006). Conditions of Preservation of Organic Materials of Vegetal Provenance in the Prehistoric Settlement at Akrotiri. *ALS Periodical Publication of the Society for the Promotion of Studies on Prehistoric Thera* **4**, 61–81.

Militello, P. (2014a). *Festòs e Haghia Triada. Rinvenimenti Minori I. Materiale per la Tessitura*. Studi di Archaeologia Cretese XI, Padova: Bottega d'Erasmo.

Militello, P. (2014b). Wool Economy in Minoan Crete before Linear B. A Minimalist Position. In C. Breniquet and C. Michel, eds., *Wool Economy in the Ancient Near East and the Aegean*, Oxford: Oxbow Books, pp. 264–282.

Milojčić, V. (1961). *Die prähistorische Siedlung unter dem Heraion: Grabung 1953 und 1955*, Bonn: Habelt.

Mina, M. (2008). *Anthropomorphic Figurines from the Neolithic and Early Bronze Age Aegean: Gender dynamics and Implications for the Understanding of Early Aegean Prehistory*, BAR International Series 1894, Oxford: British Archaeological Reports.

Möller-Wiering, S. (2006). Tools and Textiles – Texts and Contexts. Bronze Age Textiles Found in Crete, https://ctr.hum.ku.dk/research-programmes-and-projects/previous-programmes-andprojects/tools/bronze_age_textiles_found_in_crete.pdf (last accessed on March 17th 2024).

Möller-Wiering, S. (2015). External Examination of Spinning and Weaving Samples. In E. Andersson Strand and M.-L. Nosch, eds., *Tools, Textiles and Contexts: Investigating Textile Production in the Aegean and Eastern Mediterranean Bronze Age*, Oxford: Oxbow Books, pp. 101–118.

Moulhérat, C. and Spantidaki, Y. (2008). Première attestation de la laine. In C. Alfaro and L. Karali, eds., *Vestidos, Textiles Y Tintes. Estudios sobre la producción de bienes de consumo en la Antigüeadad*, València: Universitat de València, pp. 37–42.

Moulhérat, C. and Spantidaki, Y. (2009). Cloth from Kastelli Chania. *Arachne* **3**, 8–15 (English version).

Murray, S. C. (2018). Imported Exotica and Mortuary Ritual at Perati in Late Helladic IIIC East Attica. *American Journal of Archaeology* **122(1)**, 33–64.

Murray, S. C. (2023). *Long-Distance Exchange and Inter-Regional Economies*, Cambridge: Cambridge University Press. https://doi.org/10.1017/9781009319188.

Mylonas, G. E. (1972–1973). *Ο Ταφικός Κύκλος Β των Μυκηνών*, Vol. A-B, Athens: The Athens Archaeological Society.

Myres, J. L. (1950). Minoan Dress. *Man* **50**, 1–6.

Nikolakopoulou, I. (2003). Ακρωτήρι Θήρας. Η Πόλη σε Κατάσταση Έκτακτης Ανάγκης. In Α. Βλαχόπουλος και Κ. Μπίρταχα, eds., *Αργοναύτης. Τιμητικός Τόμος για τον Καθηγητή Χρίστο Γ. Ντούμα*. Αθήνα: Καθημερινή, pp. 554–573.

Nikolakopoulou, I. (2019). *Akrotiri, Thera: Middle Bronze Age Pottery and Stratigraphy, Vol. I-II*, Athens: The Athens Archaeological Society.

Nikolakopoulou, I. (2022). *Bronze Age Telos, Dodecanese*, Athens: Hellenic Organization of Cultural Resources Development.

Nordquist, G. (1987). *Asine in the Argolid: A Middle Helladic Village*, Uppsala: Academia Ubsaliensis.

Nosch, M.-L. (2012). The Textile Logograms In the Linear B Tablets. In P. Carlier, C. de Lamberterie, M. Egetmeyer, et al., eds., *Études Mycéniennes. Actes du XXXe Colloque International sur les textes Égéens. Sèvres, Paris, Nanterre, 20–23 Septembre 2010*, Roma: Fabrizio Serra Editore, pp. 303–344.

Nosch, M.-L. (2014). Mycenaean Wool Economies in the Latter Part of the 2nd Millennium BC Aegean. In C. Breniquet and C. Michel, eds., *Wool Economy in the Ancient near East and the Aegean*, Oxford: Oxbow Books, pp. 371–400.

Nosch, M.-L. (2024). Diachronic Perspectives on the Knossos Textiles (L-Series) in the Room of the Chariot Tablets, the North Entrance Passage and the Main Archival Phase. In J. Bennet, A. Karnava and T. Meißner, eds., *KO-RO-NO-WE-SA. Proceedings of the 15th international colloquium on Mycenaean studies, September 2021*, Ariadne Supplement Series 5, Rethymnon: The Faculty of Philosophy of the University of Crete, pp. 325–345.

Nosch, M.-L. and Ulanowska, A. (2021). The Materiality of the Cretan Hieroglyphic Script: Textile Production-Related Referents to Hieroglyphic Signs on Seals and Sealings from Middle Bronze Age Crete. In P. J. Boyes, P. M. Steele and N. E. Astoreca, eds., *The Social and Cultural Contexts of Historic Writing Practices*, Oxford: Oxbow Books, pp. 73–100.

Olofsson, L. (2015). An Introduction to Experimental Archaeology and Textile Research. In E. Andersson Strand and M.-L. Nosch, eds., *Tools, Textiles and*

Contexts: Investigating Textile Production in the Aegean and Eastern Mediterranean Bronze Age, Oxford: Oxbow Books, pp. 25–38.

Olofsson, L., Andersson Strand, E. and Nosch, M.-L. (2015). Experimental Testing of Bronze Age Textile Tools. In E. Andersson Strand and M.-L. Nosch, eds., *Tools, Textiles and Contexts: Investigating Textile Production in the Aegean and Eastern Mediterranean Bronze Age*, Oxford: Oxbow Books, pp. 75–100.

Overbeck, J. F. (1989). *Ayia Irini: Period IV. Part 1: The Stratigraphy and the Find Deposits. KEOS Vol. VII*, Mainz on Rhine: Philipp von Zabern.

Panagiotakopulu, E., Buckland, P. C., Day, P. M., et al. (1997). A Lepidopterous Cocoon from Thera and Evidence for Silk in the Aegean Bronze Age. *Antiquity* **71(272)**, 420–429.

Papadima, E. (2005). The Conservation of Wooden Krotala from Akrotiri, Thera. *ALS* **3**, 81–87.

Papadopoulos, S., Palli, O., Vakirtzi, S. and Psathi, E. (2018). Ayios Ioannis, Thasos: The Economy of a Small Coastal Site Dated to the Second Half of the 4th Millennium BC. In S. Dietz, F. Mavridis, Ž. Tankosić and T. Takaoğlu, eds., *Communities in Transition: The Circum-Aegean Area during the 5th and 4th Millennia BC*, Oxford: Oxbow Books, pp. 357–366.

Papageorgiou, I. (2021). The Antechamber of Xeste 3. 'The Return of the Hunters. Introductory Remarks Occasioned by Two New Wall-Paintings from Akrotiri, Thera. In C. C. Doumas and A. Devetzi, eds., *Akrotiri, Thera: Forty Years of Research (1967–2007). Scientific Colloquium, Athens, 15–16 December 2007*, Athens: Society for the Promotion of Studies on Prehistoric Thera, pp. 583–604.

Papadopoulou, E., Andersson Strand, E., Nosch, M.-L. and Cutler, J. (2015). Textile Tools from Archontiko, Northern Greece. In E. Andersson Strand and M.-L. Nosch, eds., *Tools, Textiles and Contexts: Investigating Textile Production in the Aegean and Eastern Mediterranean Bronze Age*, Oxford: Oxbow Books, pp. 293–297.

Paribeni, R. (1908). Il Sarcofago dipinto di Haghia Triada. *Monumenti Antichi* **19**, 5–86.

Pavúk, P. (2012). Of Spools and Discoid Loom-Weights: Aegean-Type Weaving at Troy Revisited. In M.-L. Nosch and R. Laffineur, eds., *KOSMOS. Jewellery, Adornment and Textiles in the Aegean Bronze Age. Proceedings of the 13th International Aegean Conference, University of Copenhagen, Danish National Research Foundation's Centre for Textile Research, 21–26 April 2010*, Leuven-Liège: Peeters, pp. 121–130.

Perlès, C. (2001). *The Early Neolithic in Greece*, Cambridge: Cambridge University Press.

Persson, A. W. (1931). *The Royal Tombs at Dendra near Midea*, Lund: C. W. K. Gleerup.

Peterson Murray, S. (2016). Patterned Textiles as Costume in Aegean Art. In M. C. Shaw and A. P. Chapin, eds., *Woven Threads: Patterned Textiles of the Aegean Bronze Age*, Oxford: Oxbow Books, pp. 43–103.

Philaniotou, O. (2019). Early Bronze Age Schematic Figurines from Thermi on Lesbos. In M. Marthari, C. Renfrew and M. J. Boyd, eds., *Beyond the Cyclades: Early Cycladic Sculpture in Context from Mainland Greece, the North and East Aegean*, Oxford: Oxbow Books, pp. 142–151.

Platon, N. (1972). Ανασκαφή Ζάκρου. *PAE* (1972), 159–192.

Popham, M. R., Betts, J. H., Cameron, M., et al. (1984). *The Minoan Unexplored Mansion at Knossos*, The British School at Athens Supplementary Volume 17, London: Thames and Hudson.

Popham, M., Touloupa, E. and Sackett, L. H. (1982). Hero of Lefkandi. *Antiquity* **56**, 169–174.

Poursat, J.-C. (1996). *Fouilles exécutées à Mallia, le quartier Mu. III: Artisans minoens: les maisons-ateliers du quartier Mu*, Études Crétoises 31, Paris: École Française d'Athènes.

Poursat, J.-C. (2012). Of Looms and Pebbles: Weaving at Minoan Coastal Settlements. In M.-L. Nosch and R. Laffineur, eds., *KOSMOS. Jewellery, Adornment and Textiles in the Aegean Bronze Age. Proceedings of the 13th International Aegean Conference, University of Copenhagen, Danish National Research Foundation's Centre for Textile Research, 21–26 April 2010*, Leuven-Liège: Peeters, pp. 31–34.

Poursat, J.-C. (2013). *Fouilles exécutées à Malia, le quartier Mu. IV: Vie quotidienne et techniques au Minoen Moyen II: Outils lithiques, poids de tissage, lampes, divers. Faune marine et Terrestre*, Études Crétoises 34, Paris: École Française d'Athènes.

Pullen, D. (2008). The Early Bronze Age in Greece. In C. Shelmerdine, ed., *The Cambridge Companion to the Aegean Bronze Age*, Cambridge: Cambridge University Press, pp. 19–46.

Rahmstorf, L. (2008). *Kleinfunde Aus Tiryns. Terrakotta, Stein, Bein und Glas/Fayence vornehmlich aus der Spätbronzezeit*, Tiryns Forschungen Und Berichte Band XVI, Wiesbaden: Dr. Ludwig Reichert Verlag Wiesbaden.

Rahmstorf, L., Siennicka, M., Andersson Strand, E. Nosch, M.-L. and Cutler, J. (2015). Textile Tools from Tiryns, Mainland Greece. In E. Andersson Strand and M.-L. Nosch, eds., *Tools, Textiles and Contexts: Investigating Textile Production in the Aegean and Eastern Mediterranean Bronze Age*, Oxford: Oxbow Books, pp. 267–278.

Rambach, J. (2000). *Kykladen I, II*, Bonn: Rudolf Habelt.

Rast-Eicher, A. (2016). *Fibres: Microscopy of Archaeological Textiles and Furs*, Budapest: Archaeolingua.

Rast-Eicher, A., Karg, S. and Bender Jørgensen, L. (2021). The Use of Local Fibres for Textiles at Neolithic Catalhoyuk. *Antiquity* **95(383)**, 1129–1144.

Rehak, P. (1996). Aegean Breechcloths, Kilts, and the Keftiu Paintings. *American Journal of Archaeology* **100**, 35–51.

Renfrew, J. (2006). The Leaf, Mat and Cloth Impressions. In L. Marangou, C. Renfrew, Ch. Doumas and G. Gavalas, eds., *Markiani on Amorgos: An Early Bronze Age Fortified Settlement. Overview of the Investigations 1987–1991*, Annual of the British School of Athens, Supplementary Volume 40, London: The British School at Athens, pp. 195–199.

Renfrew, C. (1985). *The Archaeology of Cult: The Sanctuary at Phylakopi*. BSA Supplement 18, London: The British School at Athens.

Renfrew, C. (2007). The Development of the Excavation and the Stratigraphy of Phylakopi. In C. Renfrew, N. Brodie, C. Morris and C. Scarre, eds., *Excavations at Phylakopi in Melos 1974–1977*, Supplementary Volume 42, London: The British School at Athens, pp. 5–18.

Renfrew, C. (2017) [1972]. *The Emergence of Civilisation: The Cyclades and the Aegean in the Third Millennium BC*, Oxford: Oxbow Books, 2nd ed. [Methuen 1972].

Renfrew, C., Housley, R. and Manning, S. (2006). The Absolute Dating of the Settlement. In L. Marangou, C. Renfrew, Ch. Doumas and G. Gavalas, eds., *Markiani on Amorgos: An Early Bronze Age Fortified Settlement: Overview of the Investigations 1987–1991*, Annual of the British School of Athens, Supplementary Volume 40, London: The British School at Athens, pp. 71–80.

Roach-Higgins, M. E. and Eicher, J. B. (1992). Dress and Identity. *Clothing and Textiles Research Journal* **10(4)**, 1–8.

Rougemont, F. (2014). Sheep Rearing, Wool Production and Management in Mycenaean Written Documents. In C. Breniquet and C. Michel, eds., *Wool Economy in the Ancient near East and the Aegean*, Oxford: Oxbow Books, pp. 340–370.

Ruscillo, D. (2005). Reconstructing *Murex* Royal Purple and Biblical Blue in the Aegean. In D. E. Bar-Yosef Mayer, ed., *Archaeomalacology: Molluscs in Former Environments of Human Behaviour. Proceedings of the 9th Conference of the International Council of Archaeozoology, Durham, August 2002*, Oxford: Oxbow Books, pp. 99–106.

Sakellarakis, Y. and Sapouna-Sakellaraki, E. (1997). *Archanes. Minoan Crete in a New Light*, Athens: Ammos.

Sapouna-Sakellaraki, E. (1971). *Μινωικόν Ζώμα*, Athens: The Athens Archaeological Society.

Sarpaki, A. (2007). Résultats archéobotaniques préliminaires dans divers secteurs de Malia. In M. Pomadère and J. Zurbach, eds., *Journées maliotes. Malia, ville et territoire: organization des espaces et exploitation des resources, colloque oragnisé à l'École française d'Athènes les 2 et 3 novembre 2007, Bulletin De Correspondance Hellénique* **131-2**, 882–884.

Sarri, K. (2024). The Combat Agate and the Tartan-Like Textiles of the Aegean. In U. Mannering, M.-L. Nosch, and A. Drewsen, eds., *The Common Thread: Collected Essays in Honour of Eva Andersson Strand*, Turnhout: Brepols, pp. 201–207. https://doi.org/10.1484/M.NAA-EB.5.141765.

Shaw, M. C. and Chapin, A. P. (2016). Palace and Household Textiles in Aegean Bronze Age Art. In M. C. Shaw and A. P. Chapin, eds., *Woven Threads: Patterned Textiles of the Aegean Bronze Age*, Oxford: Oxbow Books, pp. 105–130.

Sherratt, S. (2006). LH IIIC Lefkandi: An Overview. In D. Evely, ed., *Lefkandi IV. The Bronze Age. The Late Helladic IIIC Settlement at Xeropolis*, BSA Supplementary Volume 39, London: The British School at Athens, pp. 265–309.

Siennicka, M. (2020). Craftspeople, Craftsmanship and Textile Production in Early Bronze Age Greece. In L. Quillien and Kalliope Sarri, eds., *Textile Workers: Skills, Labour and Status of Textile Craftspeople between the Prehistoric Aegean and The Ancient Near East, Proceedings of the Workshop held at 10th ICAANE in Vienna, April 2016*, Vienna: Austrian Academy of Sciences, pp. 27–44.

Siennicka, M. (2023). Flax and Wool: Textile Production in Early Bronze Age Mainland Greece. In J. Banck-Burkgess, E. Marinova and D. Mischka, eds., *The Significance of Archaeological Textiles. Papers of the International Online Conference 24th–25th February 2021. THEFBO Volume II*, Esslingen: Landesamt für Denkmalpflege im Regierungspräsidium Stuttgart, pp. 141–164.

Siennicka, M. (2025). Funerary Textiles in the Prehistoric Aegean. A Case of Two Mycenaean Textile Imprints from Tomb XXI at Deiras, Argos. In E. Yvanez and M. M. Wozniak, eds., *Funerary textiles in situ: Towards a better method for the study of textile-related burial practices. Proceedings of a workshop conducted in April 2021 at the Polish Center of Mediterranean Archaeology, University of Warsaw*, Warsaw: Springer, pp. 235–251.

Siennicka, M. and Ulanowska, A. (2016). So Simple yet Universal: Contextual and Experimental Approach to Clay 'Spools' from Bronze Age Greece. In

J. Ortiz, C. Alfaro, L. Turell, and M. J. Martínez, eds., *Textiles, Basketry and Dyes in the Ancient Mediterranean World. Proceedings of the Vth International Symposium on Textiles and Dyes in the Ancient Mediterranean World (Montserrat, 19–22 March, 2014)*, València: Universidad de València, pp. 25–35.

Skals, I., Möller-Wiering S. and Nosch, M.-L. (2015). Survey of Archaeological Textile Remains from the Aegean and Eastern Mediterranean area. In E. Andersson Strand and M.-L. Nosch, eds., *Tools, Textiles and Contexts: Investigating Textile Production in the Aegean and Eastern Mediterranean Bronze Age*, Oxford: Oxbow Books, pp. 61–74.

Smith, J. S. (2012). Tapestries in the Mediterranean Late Bronze Age. In M.-L. Nosch and R. Laffineur, eds., *KOSMOS. Jewellery, Adornment and Textiles in the Aegean Bronze Age. Proceedings of the 13th International Aegean Conference, University of Copenhagen, Danish National Research Foundation's Centre for Textile Research, 21–26 April 2010*, Leuven-Liège: Peeters, pp. 241–249.

Smith, J. S. (2013). Tapestries in the Bronze and Early Iron Ages of the Ancient Near East. In M.-L. Nosch, H. Koefoed, and E. Andersson Strand, eds., *Textile Production and Consumption in the Ancient Near East: Archaeology, Epigraphy, Iconography*, Ancient Textiles Series Volume 12, Oxford: Oxbow Books, pp. 161–188.

Solazzo, C. (2019). Characterizing Historical Textiles and Clothing with Proteomics. *Conservar Património* **31**, 97–114 https://doi.org/10.14568/cp2018031.

Soriga, E. and Carannante, A. (2017). Tangled Threads: Byssus and sea silk in the Bronze Age: An Interdisciplinary Approach. In H. Landenius Enegren and F. Meo, eds., *Treasures from the Sea: Sea Silk and Shellfish Purple Dye in Antiquity*, Oxford: Oxbow Books, pp. 29-45.

Spantidaki, S. (2008). Preliminary Results on the Reconstruction of Theran Textiles. In C. Alfaro and L. Karali, eds., *Vestidos, Textiles y Tiintes: Estudios sobre la producción de bienes de consume en la Antigüedad: actas del II Symposium Internacional sobre Textiles y Tintes del Mediterráneo en el mundo antiguo (Atenas, 24 al 26 de noviembre, 2005)*, Valencia: Publicacions de la Universitat de Valencia, pp. 43–47.

Spantidaki, S. (2022). Elite Fabrics from the Grave Circles of Mycenae. *CHS Research Bulletin* **10** (2022) http://nrs.harvard.edu/URN-3:HLNC.ESSave Circle AY:102284671 (last accessed 11th March 2024).

Spantidaki, S. and Margariti, C. (2017). Archaeological Textiles Excavated in Greece. *Archaeological Reports for 2016–2017* **63**, 49–62.

Spantidaki, Y. and Moulhérat, C. (2012). Greece. In M. Gleba and U. Mannering, eds., *Textiles and Textile Production in Europe from Prehistory to AD 400*, Oxford: Oxbow Books, pp. 185–200.

Spantidaki, Y. and Moulhérat, C. (2021). Textiles at Akrotiri: Fine, Simple but not Simplistic. In C. C. Doumas and A. Devetzi, eds., *Akrotiri, Thera: Forty Years of Research (1967–2007). Scientific Colloquium, Athens, 15–16 December 2007*, Athens: Society for the Promotion of Studies on Prehistoric Thera, pp. 237–250.

Spinazzi-Lucchesi, Ch. (2018). *The Unwound Yarn: Birth and Development of Textile Tools Between Levant and Egypt*, Venezia: Edizioni Ca' Foscari, https://edizionicafoscari.unive.it/media/pdf/books/978-88-6969-251-2/978-88-6969-251-2_hdWRCFh.pdf.

Stefani, E. (2013). *Η Γυναικεία Ενδυμασία στην Ανακτορική Κρήτη*, Thessaloniki: Archaeological Institute of Macedonian and Thracian Studies.

Stocker, S. R., McNamee, C., Vitale, S., Karkanas, P. and Davis, J. L. (2022). The Grave of the Griffin Warrior at Pylos: Construction, Burial and Aftermath. *Hesperia* **91(2)**, 211–250.

Tournavitou, I., Andersson Stran, E. Nosch, M.-L. and Cutler, J. (2015). Textile Production at Mycenae, Mainland Greece. In E. Andersson Strand and M.-L. Nosch, eds., *Tools, Textiles and Contexts: Investigating Textile Production in the Aegean and Eastern Mediterranean Bronze Age*, Oxford: Oxbow Books, pp. 253–265.

Tzachili, I., Spantidaki, S., Andersson Strand, E., Nosch, M.-L. and Cutler, J. (2015). Textile Tools from Akrotiri, Thera. In E. Andersson Strand and M.-L. Nosch, eds., *Tools, Textiles and Contexts: Investigating Textile Production in the Aegean and Eastern Mediterranean Bronze Age*, Oxford: Oxbow Books, pp. 243–246.

Tzachili, I. (1990). All Important Yet Elusive: Looking for Evidence of Cloth-Making at Akrotiri. In D. A. Hardy, C. G. Doumas, J. A. Sakellarakis and P. M. Warren, eds., *Thera and the Aegean World III*, Volume One: Archaeology. London: The Thera Foundation, pp. 380–389.

Tzachili, I. (1997). *Υφαντική και Υφάντρες στο Προϊστορικό Αιγαίο*, Heraklio: Crete University Press.

Tzachili, I. (2007a). Ποικίλα. In Christos G. Doumas, ed., *Ακρωτήρι Θήρας. Δυτική Οικία. Τράπεζες-Λίθινα-Μετάλλινα-Ποικίλα*, Athens: The Athens Archaeological Society, pp. 245–282.

Tzachili, I. (2007b). Weaving at Akrotiri, Thera. Defining Cloth-Making Activities as a Social Process in a Late Bronze Age Aegean Town. In C. Gillis and M.-L. Nosch, eds., *Ancient Textiles: Production, Craft and Society*, Oxford: Oxbow Books, pp. 190–196.

Tzachili, I. (2021). New Evidence for Weaving at Akrotiri. In C. C. Doumas and A. Devetzi, eds., *Akrotiri, Thera: Forty Years of Research (1967–2007). Scientific Colloquium, Athens, 15–16 December 2007*, Athens: Society for the Promotion of Studies on Prehistoric Thera, pp. 251–255.

Tzigounaki, A. and Karnava, A. (2020). Incised and Impressed Objects from Kalo Chorafi, Mylopotamos, in Rethymno. In N. Stampolidis and M. Giannopoulou, eds., *Proceedings of the International Archaeological Conference and Symposium Eleutherna, Crete and the Outside World*, Rethymnos: University of Crete, pp. 319–328.

Tzonou-Herbst, I. (2012). Figurines. In E. H. Cline, ed., *The Oxford Handbook of the Bronze Age Aegean*, Oxford: Oxford University Press, pp. 210–222.

Ulanowska, A. (2016). Towards Methodological Principles for Experience Textile Archaeology: Experimental Approach to the Aegean Bronze Age Textile Techniques in the Institute of Archaeology, University of Warsaw. *Prilozi, Instituta za arhaeologiju u Zagrebu* **33**, 317–339.

Ulanowska, A. (2018a). In Search of 'Invisible' Textile Tools and Techniques of Band Weaving in the Bronze Age Aegean. In M. Siennicka, L. Rahmstorf and A. Ulanowska, eds., *First Textiles: The Beginnings of Textile Manufacture in Europe and the Mediterranean*, Oxford: Oxbow Books, pp. 201–212.

Ulanowska, A. (2018b). Experimenting with Loomweights: More Observations on the Functionality of Early Bronze Age Tools from Greece. In M. Siennicka, L. Rahmstorf and A. Ulanowska, eds., *First Textiles: The Beginnings of Textile Manufacture in Europe and the Mediterranean*, Oxford: Oxbow Books, pp. 201–212.

Ulanowska, A. (2020). Textile Uses in Administrative Practices in Bronze Age Greece: New Evidence of Textile Impressions from the Undersides of Clay Sealings. In M. Bustamante-Álvarez, E. H. Sánchez López and Javier Jiménez Ávila, eds., *Redefining Ancient Textile Handcraft. Structures, Tools and Production Processes. Proceedings of the VIIth International Symposium on Textiles and Dyes in the Ancient Mediterranean World (Granada, Spain 2-4 October 2019)*, Purpureae Vestes VII, Granada: Universidad de Granada, pp. 413–424.

Unruh, J. (2007). Ancient Textile Evidence in Soil Structures at the Agora Excavations in Athens, Greece. In C. Gillis and M.-L. Nosch, eds., *Ancient Textiles: Production, Craft and Society*, Oxford: Oxbow Books, pp. 167–172.

Vakirtzi, S. (2012). *Akr8794*: A Miniature Artifact from Akrotiri, Thera and the Whorl or Bead Question in the 'Whorl or Bead' Question in Light of New Textile Evidence. In M.-L. Nosch and R. Laffineur, eds., *KOSMOS. Jewellery, Adornment and Textiles in the Aegean Bronze Age. Proceedings of the 13th International Aegean Conference, University of Copenhagen,*

Danish National Research Foundation's Centre for Textile Research, 21–26 April 2010, Leuven-Liège: Peeters, pp. 215–219.

Vakirtzi, S. (2015). *Η νηματουργία στο Αιγαίο κατά την Εποχή του Χαλκού, μέσω της παρουσίας των σφονδυλιών στις αρχαιολογικές θέσεις: μελέτη της τυπολογίας, των λειτουργικών δυνατοτήτων και της διασποράς των εξαρτημάτων του αδραχτιού που βρέθηκαν σε οικισμούς και νεκροταφεία*, Unpublished Doctoral Dissertation, University of Crete.

Vakirtzi, S. (2018a). Fibre crafts and Social Complexity: Yarn Production in the Aegean Islands in the Early Bronze Age. In M. Siennicka, L. Rahmstorf and A. Ulanowska, eds., *First Textiles: The Beginnings of Textile Manufacture in Europe and the Mediterranean*, Oxford: Oxbow Books, pp. 187–200.

Vakirtzi, S. (2018b). The Thread of Life Broken: Spindles as Funerary Offerings in the Prehistoric Cyclades. *Arachne* **5**, 100–110.

Vakirtzi, S. (2019). The Loomweights. In I. Nikolakopoulou, ed., *Akrotiri, Thera: Middle Bronze Age Pottery and Stratigraphy, Vol. I-II*, Athens: The Athens Archaeological Society, pp. 485–500.

Vakirtzi, S. (2020). *Ex Oriente Ars?* 'Anatolianizing' Spindle Whorls in the Early Bronze Age Aegean Islands and their Implications for Fibre Crafts. In W. Schier and S. Pollock, eds., *The Competition of Fibres: Early Textile Production in Western Asia, South-East and Central Europe (10,000–500 BC)*, Oxford: Oxbow Books, pp. 111–126.

Vakirtzi, S. (2021). Spindle Whorls from the Recent Excavations. In C. C. Doumas and A. Devetzi, eds., *Akrotiri, Thera: Forty Years of Research (1967–2007). Scientific Colloquium, Athens, 15-16 December 2007*, Athens: Society for the Promotion of Studies on Prehistoric Thera, pp. 257–265.

Vakirtzi, S., Georma, G. and Karnava, A. (2018). Beyond Textiles: Alternative Uses of Twisted Fibres and Evidence from Akrotiri, Thera. In A. Ulanowska and M. Siennicka, eds., *Tradition and Innovation in Textile Technology in Bronze Age Europe and the Mediterranean*, Światowit Vol. LVI (2017), Warsaw: Annual of the Institute of Archaeology of the University of Warsaw, pp. 75–88.

Vakirtzi, S., Papayanni, K. and Mantzourani, E. (2022). Unwinding the Thread: Interdisciplinary Research on Early Wool Craft in Greek Prehistory. *Aura*, **5**, 153–217.

Valamoti, S. (2011). Flax in Neolithic and Bronze Age Greece: Archaeobotanical Evidence. *Vegetation History and Archaeobotany*, **20**, 549–560.

Vanden Berghe, I. (2013). Dye Analysis of Archaeological Textile Objects. In J. Banck-Burgess and C. Nübold, eds., *NESAT XI: The North European*

Symposium for Archaeological Textiles, 10–13 May 2011 in Esslingen am Neckar, Verlag Marie Leidorf GmbH, pp. 57–62.

Vlachopoulos, A. G. (2019). Η Νάξος στη Μυκηναϊκή Εποχή. In A. Angelopoulou, ed., *From Homer's World: Tenos and the Cyclades in the Mycenaean Age*, Athens: Ministry of Culture and Sports, pp. 134–144.

Vlachopoulos, A. G. (2024). *Vathy, Astypalaia: Ten Years of Research (2011–2020) on a Diachronic Palimpsest of the Aegean. Volume II. The Interdisciplinary Research*, Athens: Organization of Cultural Resources Development.

Vlasaki, M. and Hallager, E. (1995). Evidence for Seal-Use in Prepalatial Western Crete. In J.-C. Poursat and W. Müller, eds., *Sceaux minoens et mycéniens: chronologie, function et interpretation*, CMS Beiheft: 5. Berlin: Gebr. Mann Verlag, pp. 251–270.

Vogelsang-Eastwood, G. M. (1999). The Textile Impressions from Geraki. *Oxford Journal of Archaeology* **18(4)**, 371–373.

Vogelsang-Eastwood, G. M. (2000). Textiles. In P. T. Nicholson and I. Shaw, eds., *Ancient Egyptian Materials and Technology*, Cambridge: Cambridge University Press, pp. 268–298.

Wace, A. J. B., Heurtley, W. A., Lamb, W., Holland, L. B. and Boethius, C. A. (1921–1923). The Report of the School Excavations at Mycenae, 1920–1923. *The Annual of the British School at Athens* **25**, 1–434.

Warren, P. (1972). *Myrtos: An Early Bronze Age Settlement in Crete*, London: The British School At Athens.

Warren, P. (1973). The Beginnings of Minoan Religion. In G. Rizza, ed., *Antichita Cretesi: Studi in onore di Doro Levi* I, Catania: Università di Catania, pp. 37–143.

Weingarten, J. (2000). Early Helladic II Sealings from Geraki in Lakonia: Evidence for Property, Textile Manufacture and Trade. In W. Müller, ed., *Minoisch-mykenische Glyptik: Stil, Ikonographie, Funtion V*, Berlin: CMS Beiheft 6, pp. 317–329.

Weingarten, J., Crowel, J. H., Prent, M. and Vogelsang-Eastwood, G. (1999). Early Helladic Sealings from Geraki in Lakonia, Greece. *Oxford Journal of Archaeology* **18(4)**, 357–376.

de Wild, D. (2001). Appendix II: Textile Remains on Vases from Tomb 2 and Tomb 2C. In E. Karantzali, ed., *The Mycenaean Cemetery at Pylona on Rhodes*, BAR International Series 988, Oxford: Archaeopress, pp. 114–116.

Wilson, D. E. (1999). *Ayia Irini: Periods I-III. The Neolithic and Early Bronze Age Settlements. Part 1: The Pottery and Small Finds*, KEOS IX, Mainz on Rhine: Philipp Von Zabern.

Wisti-Lassen, A. (2015). Weaving with Crescent Shaped Loom Weights. An Investigation of a Special Kind of Loom Weight. In In E. Andersson Strand and M.-L. Nosch, eds., *Tools, Textiles and Contexts: Investigating Textile Production in the Aegean and Eastern Mediterranean Bronze Age*, Oxford: Oxbow Books, 127–137.

Wright, J. C. (2008). Early Mycenaean Greece. In C. W. Shelmerdine, ed., *The Cambridge Companion to the Aegean Bronze Age*, New York: Cambridge University Press, pp. 230–257.

Zavadil, M. (2023). Spinnschüsseln am giechischen Festland: Faktum oder Fiktion? In U. Lohner-Urban, W. Spickermann and E. Trinkl, eds., *Itineraria. II> Rund ums Mittelmeer. Festschrift für Peter Scherrer zum 65. Geburtstag. Keryx 10*, Graz: Unipress Verlag, pp. 313–325.

Zora, P. (1956). *Τα Πολυτελή Φορέματα των Κρητομυκηναίων Κυριών*. Athens.

Acknowledgements

I would like to thank the editors of the series 'The Aegean Bronze Age' for inviting me to contribute this Element on Aegean Bronze Age textile craft. Thanks are due to Dr K. Nikolentzos, Head of the Prehistoric Collection, and Dr G. Moraitou, Head of the Department of Conservation, Chemical and Physical Research and Archaeometry of the National Archaeological Museum for granting me permission to examine the mineralized cloth fragment on the EBA dagger of Dokathismata. Also, to Dr E. Gerontakou for discussing with me the textile fragments of Zakros. Many thanks are extended to the Ephorates, Museums and Excavation archives of the Hellenic Ministry of Culture, ODAP, the Athens Archaeological Society, Akrotiri Excavations, Foreign Schools in Athens, CMS Heidelberg, Classics Department/University of Cincinnati, as well as individuals/copyright holders who generously gave permission to use the images of this Element. Warm thanks to V. Papazikou who helped me with the drawings. This Element benefitted considerably from the feedback provided by two anonymous reviewers. Any remaining shortcomings are my own.

Cambridge Elements =

The Aegean Bronze Age

Carl Knappett
University of Toronto
Carl Knappett is the Walter Graham/ Homer Thompson Chair in Aegean Prehistory at the University of Toronto.

Irene Nikolakopoulou
Hellenic Ministry of Culture, Archaeological Museum of Heraklion
Irene Nikolakopoulou is an archaeologist and curator at the Archaeological Museum of Heraklion, Crete.

About the Series
This series is devised thematically to foreground the conceptual developments in the Aegean Bronze Age, one of the richest subfields of archaeology, while reflecting the range of institutional settings in which research in this field is conducted. It aims to produce an innovative and comprehensive review of the latest scholarship in Aegean prehistory.

Cambridge Elements⁼

The Aegean Bronze Age

Elements in the Series

Long-Distance Exchange and Inter-Regional Economies
Sarah C. Murray

Aegeomania: Modern Reimaginings of the Aegean Bronze Age
Nicoletta Momigliano

Economy and Commodity Production in the Aegean Bronze Age
Catherine E. Pratt

The Emergence of Aegean Prehistory
Andrew Shapland

Clothing Bodies: Weaving and Textiles in the Aegean Bronze Age
Sophia Vakirtzi

A full series listing is available at: www.cambridge.org/EABA

For EU product safety concerns, contact us at Calle de José Abascal, 56–1º, 28003 Madrid, Spain or eugpsr@cambridge.org.

www.ingramcontent.com/pod-product-compliance
Ingram Content Group UK Ltd.
Pitfield, Milton Keynes, MK11 3LW, UK
UKHW022150150326
469019UK00020B/1598